No Stupid Question

We struggle with imperfect knowledge and the pain of sin in this life – but with God there are no stupid questions: just abundant grace in Christ.

In the UK, the new academic year always begins in September. As we meet the new students, who are excited to begin their journey into the mission and ministry to which God has called them, we often tell them that there are no stupid questions. If there is something they don't understand then they shouldn't hold back for fear of appearing silly! College is a place to learn and to grow in the knowledge and love of God, and in fact we learn and grow the most through our mistakes and the things that go wrong.

In our readings this quarter I was especially struck by the 'bumpy' way in which David grows into his God-given kingship. Far from being a perfect character, David comes to us in glorious technicolour with all his flaws visible. We have an 'outsider' perspective on David through the Bible's historical books, and a more personal angle from the psalms attributed to him. From these sources we see him fail and repent and then start again, and in this he is a hero with whom we can identify. We see David's torment as he realises all that he is not - and laments his weakness.

Followers of Jesus are called to grow into the image of Jesus Christ (eg Romans 8:29), who is himself the image of God (Colossians 1:15). This King is truly without comparison and beyond reproach, a glorious and undeserved destiny for men and women. We grow not in our own strength but by standing humbly under the cross of Christ, with our failings, our sin and our 'stupid questions' - which are not really stupid at all, but part of our human pilgrimage. There is always a new start in him.

May the readings this quarter encourage you on your journey into Christ and show you more of his glory each day.

Sally Nelson
Editor

Annabel Moule
Content Assistant

ON THE COVER: **Mary Evans explores how the messages of the Old Testament prophets are relevant today, giving us a clearer understanding of who Jesus is.**

Image credit: Shutterstock / fran_kie

The Writers

ANDY ROBINSON has served as a church minister, author and evangelist. His love for preaching, alongside a call to minister, led him to Moorlands College. He has spent nearly a decade as a pastor and travels the country sharing his story and seeing God change lives.

DANIEL MCGINNIS is the Vice Principal of St Hild College and leads the Barnabas Teaching Centre in Sheffield. He is also the Executive Director of the Leeds School of Theology. He loves the books of Luke and Acts, and has a passion for seeing today's church inspired by the earliest church. He also enjoys teaching theology, particularly New Testament studies and hermeneutics.

TANYA FERDINANDUSZ and her husband Roshan have been married for over 25 years and have two adult sons – Daniel and Joshua. Tanya is both a freelance writer and freelance editor, and she has been writing Bible reading notes, articles and devotionals for over 20 years. She is the author of Marriage Matters, a book for Christian couples.

MARY EVANS is a former theological lecturer, still involved with research supervision and marking. Writing, speaking, church family, friends and Langham Partnership Board responsibilities fill much of the rest of available time.

JONNY LIBBY is a Lay Pastor for Plymouth Methodist Central Hall. This role includes being the Methodist Chaplain at Plymouth University.

SALLY NELSON is the Dean of Baptist Formation at St Hild College, Yorkshire, UK, where she also teaches Christian doctrine and pastoral care. She is a Baptist minister and has been the commissioning editor for Encounter with God since 2015.

ANNABEL MOULE is a Content Assistant at Scripture Union and the content manager for Encounter with God. She studied English Literature at Oxford Brookes University and Theology at the University of Oxford. She lives in Bath and is recently married to Henry.

Contents

This edition of *Encounter with God* copyright © Scripture Union 2022
ISSN 1350-5130. All rights reserved.

Scripture Union is a member of the worldwide Scripture Union international community.
Website: https://scriptureunion.global

CATCHING THE BIBLE BUG

Alison Pickering shares how Scripture Union's *Diary of a Disciple* is opening up the Bible and getting children to read it regularly – even those with no church background. And, as she explains, the impact has been amazing!

Alison works for outreach charity The Urban Family. For 15 years, she had run weekly clubs, partnering with four North West London churches, with the aim of introducing non-church children to Jesus. She had also been using SU's *Diary of a Disciple: Luke's Story* in a discipleship group of three children from another church, and they loved it.

So, when the pandemic came and, with it, the first national lockdown, Alison decided to set up an online club to include the children without church backgrounds too, and use *Diary of a Disciple* as its basis.

'We got a copy of the book to each child. Originally, I'd planned to read a short extract to them each day, but they were so keen that things quickly evolved! So, from March to July 2020, we had a 45-minute afternoon slot, Monday to Friday, which we called *Live at Five*. We'd start with a prayer and a couple of worship songs, a game of some sort and then we would read a page or two of Luke's story from the *Diary of a Disciple* books. Finally, I would give a short talk. Every Saturday, we'd have a session to review what we'd learned during the week.'

Children couldn't put *Diary of a Disciple* down

Most of the children never went to church and had never picked up a Bible before, let alone read one. 'They didn't know the Gospel of Luke at all,' Alison says. 'But at our online gatherings, the children were vying to get to read the next part of *Diary of a Disciple* out loud to the rest of the group.'

'Their parents were so grateful that we were encouraging their children's reading, because in many cases their reading levels had plummeted over lockdown. They were telling me how well written *Diary of a Disciple* was, how their child loved it so much that they couldn't put it down.

'Amelia was one of the few children in the group who was from a church family. Her mum told me how she'd tried for years to get Amelia to read the Bible regularly, to no avail. But now her daughter was telling her, "Mummy, I've got to spend time every day reading my Bible" – and off she would go! The children who weren't from church families were just as enthusiastic, telling me how they were sitting down and reading it cover to cover. Over the months, it became a habit for them – hopefully a habit that will last.'

Having finished Luke's story, the group started reading the next *Diary of a Disciple* book on the lives of Peter and Paul. Alison comments, 'I love these books. I've learned from reading them too, and I hope some day children will be able to read the whole Bible in this *Diary of a Disciple* format.'

The children who weren't from church families were just as enthusiastic...

Every child wanted to share and pray

Diary of a Disciple and the *Live at Five* online club has really helped Alison to engage with the children on unprecedented levels. She says, 'My personal experience of working with children over the past twenty years has been that if I ask someone to pray out loud, the room suddenly falls silent. 'Not any more! Increasingly, the children wanted to be able to pray for our protection and our needs, and to share what God was doing in their lives. Thursdays became 'Thoughtful Thursdays' – in the first 15 minutes of the session, children would take it in turns to share just one thing they were grateful to God for. Every child always had something to be grateful for, and all of them wanted to share.'

A doubling of numbers

The group of families grew quickly. On the first day in March 2020, there were 15 families, but three months later, 25 families were joining in, most on a daily basis. Alison comments,

'Going online opened up the freedom for children to invite cousins or friends. Some of them moved schools the following autumn and invited their new school friends.

Increasingly, the children wanted to be able to pray for our protection and our needs, and to share what God was doing in their lives.

'The group grew and grew. Now we have around 50 families in all – over a dozen of them from outside London! We just post a copy of *Diary of a Disciple* to them, it's easy enough to do. When the children returned to lessons in the classroom in September of 2020, we reduced *Live at Five* to one session a week. Nevertheless, most of the children still continue to come on the online sessions regularly.'

Now Ben just loves Jesus!

Alison recalls the spiritual journey of one young man in the online group. 'Ben who was ten had started coming to the kid's club we used to run before lockdown. His family weren't Christians and he'd never read a Bible in his life, he had no understanding of it. When we started up *Live at Five* on Zoom and reading *Diary of a Disciple*, he'd be there every day. And he loved it – he was the first child in our group to realise that what he was reading about in *Diary of a Disciple* was relevant to his own life today. 'Now Ben just loves Jesus! And he longs for his family to get to know Jesus too. When he came on our summer camp this year, Ben was asking us to pray for them.'

The holiday club will help children catch the Bible bug!

Now, Scripture Union has launched a new *Diary of a Disciple Holiday Club*, aimed particularly at children who don't have a church background. Alison thinks it's a great idea. 'From my own experience, *Diary of a Disciple* really brings the Bible to life for children without church backgrounds. They love the stories, and it really helps them 'get' who Jesus is. So, I hope and pray that it will help many more children like Ben to discover Jesus, to understand his message, and to follow him.' Find out more about the Diary of a Disciple holiday club resource at su.org.uk/diaryclub

A shorter version of this story first appeared in *Connecting You*, SU's free quarterly supporter magazine, in Winter 2021. If you'd like to receive copies of *Connecting You* and learn more of how God is moving in the hearts and lives of children and young people today, you can sign up online at su.org.uk/connectingyou.

Using this Guide

Encounter with God is designed for thinking Christians who want to interpret and apply the Bible in a way that is relevant to the problems and issues of today's world. It is based on the NIV translation of the Bible, but can easily be used with any other version.

Each set of readings begins with an *Introduction* to the section you are about to study. The *Call to Worship* section at the start of each note should help you consciously to come into God's presence before you read the passage. The main *Explore* section aims to bring out the riches hidden in the text. The *Growing in Faith* section at the end suggests ways of applying the message to daily living.

The *Bible in a Year* readings at the foot of the page are for those who want this additional option.

EARTHLY KINGS AND HEAVENLY REALMS

These passages offer timeless, daily challenges, as we read how individual choices affect whole families, their legacies and their relationships: choices which lead to murder, betrayal, love, envy – it is all here. With cautionary hindsight, we witness mighty men rise and fall, we see human strength emboldened by God or totally quashed by him. We witness human self-seeking in preference to seeking God's heart and how those with great potential can rise and fall.

As disciples, we understand the complexity of daily choices, but that is compounded here by promises of power and untold wealth. We are challenged to keep focused on the eternal, to avoid turning our eyes to the immediate glitter. Every story has two sides and these are no exception – Saul, who reigned for so long, fades disappointingly in comparison to David, the shepherd boy. Through David, God saw fit to establish an earthly throne of enormous influence and power and to go beyond David's comprehension by declaring that this was the never-ending kingdom.

The messianic throne of David would become clearer as the ages passed, revealed through a king who would leave everlasting glory to be born in a lowly place, to be crowned with thorns and to die. While other kings came and went, God was establishing a new kingdom built on decades of faithful servants, many of whom struggled and seemed insignificant. When they handed that insignificance to God and walked with him, when they obeyed God before their own desires, God revealed himself. We will read of changing kings and kingdoms, of divided houses being reunited, but what never has, or will, change is the overriding narrative throughout this story (and all stories): the King of kings is the one who has been, who will be and who always is to come.

Andy Robinson

FOR FURTHER READING

David Tsumura, *NICOT The Second Book of Samuel*, Eerdmans, 2019
K Chafin, *The Preacher's Commentary, 1 & 2 Samuel*, Thomas Nelson, 1989
R Alter, *The David Story: A Translation with Commentary of 1 and 2 Samuel*, WW Norton, 2000

2 Samuel 3:6–39

The Author Pens the Story

'Not that I have already ... arrived at my goal, but I press on to take hold of that for which Christ Jesus took hold of me.'[1]

My dog has huge brown eyes, which he uses to great effect when he wants something, or to make you feel guilty! We, too, learn how to manipulate others for our own ends. Today's reading shows us a time when lives and legacies depended on sides, loyalty and wise decisions in leadership. Abner initially makes it clear he is loyal – today! – to the house of Saul (v 8). Having made Ish-Bosheth into a puppet king, he would have lived obediently under him and may have even desired the throne himself but, as Abner is accused of this sexual act of treason,[2] it encourages him to revolt!

Abner shifts his loyalty, looking to make a union with David, bringing together the houses of Israel and Judah (v 10) – God's desired outcome. We may often question how God can possibly be involved in – or aware of – our situations or church life, because of the way they unfold. But God is in control. We have read how all opposition to David from Saul to Abner was removed from his path. God has, as expected, clearly gone before David. David hasn't murdered or manipulated. Rather he has (albeit strategically at times) honoured his opposers, resulting in restoration and unity between the factions, a halt to bloodshed and joint affirmation of David's actions and leadership (v 36).

Now, for the first time, we read the messianic phrase 'the throne of David' (v 10, ESV).[3] God has placed David on the throne as he intended. What a challenge when all seems impossible, that God *is* working, for as God declares: 'my thoughts are not your thoughts, neither are your ways my ways'.[4] Throughout history, many have and will continue to give him thanks for that fact and for his ultimate perfect timing and intervention.

'...he who began a good work in you will carry it on to completion'!⁵ Are you willing to trust him when this looks far from reality?

---

[1] Phil 3:12 [2] Taking the concubine of a late monarch was seen as a bid for the throne, 2 Sam 16:22 [3] See eg Luke 1:32 [4] Isa 55:8 [5] Phil 1:6

BIBLE IN A YEAR: **2 Chronicles 33,34; Psalms 75,76**

Integrity of Heart

Lord, help me to read and respond to today's words with honesty and integrity. Lord, keep me focused on your holiness; Lord, I need to confess before you...

Another murder, another killing! It's difficult reading of violent act after violent act. Such acts, even though extreme, displayed the work of the enemy – and today, also, the sinful nature which controls so many of our own desires and actions. We cannot judge others. As Paul declared, all of us have fallen short and sinned before God.[1] Thankfully, when we seek the Lord with all our heart and in repentance, salvation flows freely.

Notice that Ish-Bosheth was *murdered* (v 11, GNB), whereas David's act is described as *killing* (v 12), an important distinction: one is unjust, the other just. David, throughout our readings, refuses to be associated with any actions that would contradict his master – the living God. Unsurprisingly then, when he is brought Ish-Bosheth's head (as with Saul's death), he is not grateful but incensed that others would insult his integrity as a man of God. David shows great consistency and the Lord himself sees this in advising Solomon later: 'if you walk before me faithfully with integrity of heart and uprightness, as David your father did, and do all I command and observe my decrees and laws, I will establish your royal throne over Israel for ever, as I promised David your father'.[2] Are we serving the Lord with wholehearted integrity, seeking glory for him alone, or are we searching for more for ourselves, more power and control over others? Beware, for this account reminds us of a God who clearly looks into and knows our hearts and acts with unswerving holy righteousness.

Think through your relationships, especially online ones. Are you using anyone to elevate yourself? What safeguards and accountabilities do you have in place to protect your integrity?

[1] Rom 3:23 [2] 1 Kings 9:4,5

BIBLE IN A YEAR: **2 Chronicles 35,36; Luke 1:39–80**

Psalm 52

Oaks of Righteousness

'Beauty for ashes, joy instead of mourning, praise instead of despair ... they will be called oaks of righteousness, a planting of the Lord for the display of his splendour.'[1]

David is incandescent with rage and his emotion is expressed with honesty through his gifts of music and writing. The psalm is then passed on to the community for corporate response and interpretation. Here we can see why the psalms are so precious to us. The emotions expressed are common to us all. The highs we often expect, the lows stir up all manner of responses.

David is angry that injustice still reigns, that just because he had consulted the priests at Nob, they were unnecessarily slaughtered.[2] Saul had lost control. His growing envy, jealousy and determination to succeed without God are in contrast with David's character. David was witnessing an evil reign and his remark, 'Why do you boast ... mighty hero?' (v 1) is scathing, for what mighty warrior slaughters 85 gowned priests? and their whole town?[3] Whether David is talking of Saul or Doeg or both is unknown, but there is little to separate them. Jesus said that a tree is recognisable by its fruit[4] and David substantiates the point. The evil ones will be uprooted, facing everlasting destruction (v 5), whereas David, depicted as an olive tree, signifies security, well-being and deep roots. David's dismay and anger are well-founded, but he must make the same choice as we must in the face of injustice: to trust in the Lord, but also to bear righteous fruit, to act in line with God-given principles. David hopes for vindication in the future, but vengeance is not his. He is to serve, as he is commanded, to follow as the Lord leads. Saul has trusted in wealth, power and evil – earthly temporal fantasies, whereas David can flourish in spite of injustice, for God is trustworthy in unfailing love. To hope in his name is to live eternally (vs 8,9).

How do we respond to the injustice around us? Are we acting, speaking and standing on God's Word, or simply walking by?

---

[1] Isa 61:3, paraphrased [2] 1 Sam 22:6-23 [3] 1 Sam 22:18,19 [4] Matt 7:20

BIBLE IN A YEAR: **Ezra 1,2; Luke 2**

The One True King

Praise him, because even today after generations of faithfulness, God has not changed and is here. 'Lord, you have been our dwelling-place throughout all generations.'[1]

Long ago, I left theological college with a heart on fire for Jesus and my new church – and with the arrogance of assuming 'it's all right now, church, I've arrived!' Much of that was the naivety of new beginnings, together with a great passion for God and a desire to see his kingdom come and people saved. However, although God had called and partly equipped me, he did not *need* me to bring his plan to fruition. More than anything I could ever achieve, he wanted a relationship with me.

Today, as we encounter this principle in David's life, it's easy to see, first, only David's achievements: the anointed king, the conquering of Jerusalem for his capital, the enemy defeated. This, however, would be to miss seeing the true King over all. God doesn't call David 'king': he calls him 'shepherd' and the ruler of his people Israel (v 2). They are

God's people and they are the ones who can anoint David king, but God is the King of kings and David knew that (v 12). David was to continue as shepherd, for God had anointed and positioned him, as he had Saul.

Saul may have ruled for 42 years, David for 40, yet whose legacy was most prominent? David grew in power because God was with him (v 10), the *relationship* was fostered in psalmist as well as soldier (something Saul had abandoned). David humbly honoured that relationship above all others. God had once again used his servants on earth to bring his people back together. This is not about making a king but uniting the fractured fragments: 'All the tribes of Israel came' (v 1). Our God is always seeking to restore and bring his people into unity and loving relationship as family with him, the true Shepherd King.

Lord, forgive me when I see my worth as being in actions or ministry, rather than in the loving relationship we have. I commit my life again into your hands.

[1] Ps 90:1

2 Samuel 6

Zion – My Dwelling Place

Lord, still my busy life and my thoughts. Lord, touch my heart as I reach out to touch you. In your holy presence, I bow before you.

David has conquered Jerusalem: henceforth, it stands as political centre for the new united people of Israel. Now he moves to make it the religious centre too. It has been 20 years since the Philistines returned the Ark[1] – and David wanted it home: 'For the LORD has chosen Zion, he has desired it for his dwelling'.[2] The Ark's arrival in Jerusalem is a climactic moment in the religious history of the Israelites: from now on the Lord would place his name in Jerusalem.[3]

It may be hard for us to see the full importance of this event. Yet Uzzah's death reveals a stark reality (v 7). David had not taken the Ark into the battle for Jerusalem, perhaps demonstrating his feeling that the Ark was *only* symbolic. However, his decision to bring it home reveals a thin division between symbol and reality. For Christians today, baptism and communion are indeed

symbolic, but to treat them *only* as symbols is to treat the Lord's presence with a dangerous familiarity. God had made clear his instructions for moving the Ark (to carry it using the poles).[4] Here, the people deviated from God's instructions. Yet God isn't intermittently just or unjust. The laws he gave were for the people's protection. David reacted with anger initially; this was followed by understandable measures (v 10). The Ark, however symbolic, represented the presence of the Lord and was to be honoured and treated as holy. I am drawn to reflect on Calvary: the cross is symbolic *and* totally mysterious, because it allows us to reach out to God, as Uzzah could not. I can stand in God's presence without fear because of Jesus. Yet that freedom, illuminated through this passage, reminds us that God is still holy and it is only by grace that we enter his presence.

Read Psalm 132, reflecting on the captivating promises and lavish blessings as the bridegroom sings over his bride, his people, and over you today.

---

[1] 1 Sam 7:2 [2] Ps 132:13 [3] David Tsumura, *NICOT The Second book of Samuel*, Eerdmans, 2019, p106 [4] Exod 25:14

BIBLE IN A YEAR: **Ezra 5,6; Psalm 77**

When God says 'No'!

Lord, I lay before you all my plans, my heart's desires for you and my family. Lord, open my heart to hear all your words, even the hard ones.

Nathan is represented as a faithful servant, a man of God. Giving words of affirmation to people is a beautiful gift, yet undertaking the opposite is challenging. For all prophets, to speak words from God with integrity inevitably means delivering a message that runs counter to man's heart. Nathan bravely and humbly returns to the king and shares the word of the Lord (v 17; 'But...', v 4), which is in complete contrast to his first statement (v 3). One was his thought, the other the Lord's instruction!

In those times, to face kings with bad news could cost your life, as history has shown over generations. We know David's heart was for God, but we can change when circumstances no longer please us. Ultimately, Nathan was prepared to say, 'God says "No"'. That is a hard statement to make – and to take. Often we have great plans and visions in God's service and it hurts when others disagree, or interject with practicalities, or tell us to wait.

Nathan also has a promise to share, for God is preparing David for far more than temples in earthly realms. This is of messianic and supernatural proportions (v 13). As God declares 'I AM', look again and see what God will do for David and his people: 'I took you from the pasture ... I have been with you ... I will make your name great' (vs 8,9) ... I will provide for my people, give you rest, raise up your offspring, establish his kingdom, be his father, punish him when he does wrong, but never stop loving him as I did Saul (vs 10–15). These are not temporal promises for one man (v 16), but to all God's people, promises that will endure for ever. What joy, hope and protection!

'I will go before you and will level the mountains; I will break down gates of bronze and cut through bars of iron.'[1] Are we trusting ourselves, or God?

[1] Isa 45:2

2 Samuel 7:18–29

Is this Normal, Lord?

We praise and thank you today, Lord, for the blessings and gifts you provide. Forgive our focus on the internal (or material), over your eternal fragrance poured over us.

Yesterday we heard the great I AM speaking with promise and lavishness over David. Today we have that leader broken before God, saying, 'Who am I?' (v 18). David is but a servant before God (v 20), something he always has been, but he is now bowed down by the enormity of God, not just for Israel but in his life and legacy. Man may say, 'Nothing lasts for ever'. God disagrees. David's kingdom in God's hand would be eternal (v 29). Our *own* kingdoms, business and even families will not last for ever, but Jesus will. The greatest privilege of our lives is asking God to show us where we can join him.[1] This covenant is so lavish that David unsurprisingly questions: 'Is this your usual way of dealing with man...?' (v 19, NIV 1983 edition). It is undeserved love, amazing grace. Once more God has chosen the least: Saul from the smallest tribe, David the smallest son – or Nazareth the place from which nothing good could come.[2] Repeatedly, we see God using the weak to shame the strong,[3] thereby illuminating his greatness in them.

What a promise to us! The everlasting kingdom spans the generations, touching those of us who have been so far from the kingdom – yet God, for some utterly incredible reason, reaches down and gives us more than we could ever expect or appreciate. The challenge is to look afresh, to 'See what great love the Father has lavished on us, that we should be called children of God! And that is what we are!'[4] I don't deserve it, but I have received it. Or perhaps, over time, have we switched our eyes from Jesus to the world, its problems, worries and ills?

Turn your eyes upon Jesus, look full in his wonderful face; let earthly worries grow dim, as his glory and beauty fill you, not just today but for evermore![5]

[1] JD Greear and others, *1 & 2 Samuel*, Holman, 2016, p176 [2] John 1:46 [3] 1 Cor 1:27 [4] 1 John 3:1 [5] From H Lemmel, 'Turn Your Eyes Upon Jesus', 1922

BIBLE IN A YEAR: **Ezra 9,10; Luke 5**

The Unstoppable Force!

'Search me, God, and know my heart; test me and know my anxious thoughts. See if there is any offensive way in me, and lead me in the way everlasting.'[1]

Revisiting the barbaric events in this passage through our modern lens is difficult. However, we must read as beneficiaries of them, while we balance our disquiet. This text stands as a capstone to David's great reign. Together with the capture of Jerusalem (chs 5-6) and the dynastic promise (ch 7), these verses produce a portrait of an Israelite kingdom that captures the imagination of subsequent generations.[2] We must view these events as the chronicler does, but without circumnavigating the tough questions, even if an answer is unlikely. How could God allow such things? Worse still, command and control such acts? Saul faced justice, as do others, yet evil *still* prospers and many still endlessly suffer through mankind's selfish desires. God alone is truly just and will bring judgement. Meanwhile, as disciples, we are called to bring his light into the darkness.

Here we see a man anointed by God in ways which meant that no enemy plan or terror could halt him in his pursuit of what God was doing through him. The narrator shows David's great victories over all who stood against him, but the overriding narrative is that this is because of God's anointing. This is the difference between Saul and David. David's obedience to God's commands reinforces what God truly requires of us (v 15).[3] God had promised David, and therefore his people, rest from their enemies and peace on the borders.[4] David is the embodiment of the Lord's rule on earth, the Lord who would defeat death's valley (which was never his intention for us) and lead us into conflict-free, green pastures.[5] As we face another day, whether in green pastures or death's valley, we can trust that this everlasting kingdom fulfilled in Jesus has come near.

The kingdom is near. We can be still, knowing that he *is* God.[6] He is leading us to peace and victory. No weapon forged against us can prevail.[7]

---

[1] Ps 139:23,24   [2] Bill Arnold, *NIV Commentary, 1 & 2 Samuel*, Zondervan, 2003, p493   [3] Mic 6:8
[4] 2 Sam 7:11   [5] Ps 23   [6] Ps 46:10   [7] Isa 54:17

BIBLE IN A YEAR: **Nehemiah 1,2; Psalm 78:1–37**

2 Samuel 9

Welcome to the Banquet

'Amazing grace! How sweet the sound / that saved a wretch like me.'[1] Thank you, Jesus, for bringing me out of the pit and setting my feet on your rock.

Personally, having experienced years of painful suffering, sometimes feeling like 'a dead dog' is a true expression of reality (v 8). Whether Mephibosheth said that to show homage before David is unclear, but it's a powerful picture. His father was Jonathan and his grandfather, Saul. Having once lived in a king's house, he was now before one who could humiliate or kill him. Years before, when Mephibosheth was just five, David had promised unfailing love to Jonathan's family[2] and Mephibosheth is now an adult. No doubt terrified, he is welcomed into the king's throne room. In a reflection of God's goodness to him, David restores the lands to Mephibosheth's family, setting people around him to provide for his needs, even inviting him to dine at the king's table (vs 7,11).

The parallels cry out to us from this story. That we, who were but broken pieces laid before the King, would be restored as *heirs*. More than that, to be welcomed into the King's presence, by name. Not meeting with the expected (and just) death sentence, but finding a welcome of the greatest proportion and honour – and the restoration of all the enemy has taken from us! Ziba calls him the lame son (v 3), the king calls him by name (v 6) and adopts him as family. In the same way, God invites us personally into restoration and relationship. In redemption we find blessings beyond comprehension, even everlasting life and the joy of being his children. Just as the disciples sat sharing with the Lord, we are invited to the King's feast! Psalm 23 expresses it beautifully: he prepares a table for us before our enemies, we are to be anointed and dwelling in God's house for ever.[3] Or, as David's son described it, 'Let him lead me to the banquet hall, and let his banner over me be love.'[4]

Who are we inviting to the feast, to receive God's grace and eternal love?

[1] John Newton, 1779 [2] 1 Sam 20:14–17 [3] Ps 23:5 [4] Song 2:4

BIBLE IN A YEAR: **Nehemiah 3,4; Luke 6**

Am I Foolish?

Lord, open my heart to the truth within. Open my eyes and teach me today how to trust you in a deeper, unseen yet assured way. Amen.

I often dread the thing that never happens (v 5)! Ultimately, what do we fear: life after death, life without God? Calvary covers them all. David did not know that, but he still saw the day of rejoicing and salvation coming. This psalm no doubt identifies with those who should have known better yet turned from God with flagrant disregard (v 4)! How often I say (without *actually* saying it), 'There is no God'. My sinful acts are a disregard of God, unlikely to be performed were he fully visible before me. My dismissal of his voice is blatant denial of his presence.

For David, living amongst those with constant antagonism towards God was hard, as though 'everyone has turned away' (v 3) and no one was left. How easy it is to be like Elisha's servant, seeing only the army which is against us. Yet, as Elisha said, 'Those who are with us are more than those who are with them.'[1] Today we still feel this, as though everyone has rejected God and we walk alone. We, too, must be wary of exaggerated generalisations – 'no one cares', 'everyone in church' thinks this or that – and of self-prominence or self-victimisation. Fact: God is Most High and therefore sees all (v 2) and he acts accordingly. David's prayer *is* heard and answered: 'Oh, that salvation … would come out of Zion!' (v 6). Jesus Christ has come and is coming, as Scripture rejoices: 'Daughter Zion … See, your king comes to you'.[2] So, rejoice, be glad, say and fear what you will, but be aware – only the fool says in his heart, 'There is no God' (v 1). Maybe not instantly, or in the way we expect, but Israel *will* rejoice, as will Jacob, as God hears and the cry (v 6) is answered.

Beware of the enemy's ploy – to say 'there is no God'. God is victorious; everything is his and under his authority. We rest in that blessed assurance.

[1] 2 Kings 6:16 [2] Matt 21:5; see also Zech 9:9

BIBLE IN A YEAR: **Nehemiah 5,6; Luke 7**

Luke 3–9

PREPARATION AND MINISTRY IN GALILEE

Luke's Gospel is the longest book in the New Testament, a masterfully written narrative of the life, death and resurrection of Jesus. The synoptic Gospels of Matthew, Mark and Luke are very similar, but each has a unique contribution and a distinctive emphasis. We will encounter Luke's characteristic themes in the coming chapters, including: (1) the universal inclusion of all people and the recognition of the central part Gentiles play in God's plan; (2) an emphasis on the importance of regular prayer and, particularly, Jesus' habit of praying before important occasions; (3) a focus on the significant role of women in the Jesus movement; (4) a special interest in the poor and the marginalised, including the social ostracism they suffer; (5) a concern for 'sinners', who are often juxtaposed favourably against religious leaders; (6) a stress on the family circle and the use of familial settings and imagery.

Our readings start with a focus on Jesus' preparation for ministry (3:1 – 4:13). The next chapters are Luke's stories of Jesus' ministry in his home regions, in Galilee (4:14 – 9:50). This section is filled with memorable miracles and preaching, with a few parables sprinkled here and there. Luke's main theme throughout is the nature of Jesus' Messiahship and mission.

As you study this central portion of Luke's Gospel, watch for the themes mentioned above and allow them to shape your own devotional life and outlook. Because this material is narrative, pay close attention to the plot, the various characters and settings, the overall structure and the repeated themes. Luke has written these vivid episodes to make a profound impact on the reader; his goal is to inspire and to provoke. This is transformative, though not always comfortable. May our hearts be open to being formed and renovated by these stories as we read and ponder them.

Daniel McGinnis

FOR FURTHER READING

Two of the best commentaries on Luke's Gospel are Bock's *Baker Exegetical Commentary on the New Testament* and Nolland's *Word Biblical Commentary*; these will inform the background of the following notes.

Luke 3:1–20

Wilderness Makes the Way

God of desert places, open our hearts to the beauty and opportunity found in the wilderness.

Today's passage focuses on the role of John the Baptist, who sets the scene for Jesus' coming ministry. John has grown up in a rural area and Luke emphasises his connection to the wilderness (vs 2–4).[1] It was not uncommon for prophets to use the isolation of uninhabited desert places to cultivate a deeper spiritual life, separate from and uninfluenced by economic and political powers as well as hypocritical religious leaders. They could then prophesy, with personal authority and God's power, against such systems and institutions. John's message is as rugged and uncompromising as his environment, focused on God's judgement and the need for repentance.

The phrase 'in the wilderness' refers back to Isaiah,[2] as quoted in verses 4–6, and to Abraham's and Moses' encounters with God in the wilderness. The wilderness has been a crucial part of the journey of God's people throughout Scripture and throughout history. In fact, it is the place in which the prophetic message is formed and birthed, for it prepares the way for God to move in and through his people. John's experience in the wilderness prepares him for his prophetic ministry (v 2), which in turn prepares the way for the life and ministry of Jesus the Messiah (vs 15–17). This time in the desert allows John to recognise Jesus and his coming baptism with the Holy Spirit and with fire. The harshness of the wilderness, with its stripping back, heat and scarcity, is often the place where we find God.

Personally, I've been in a painful wilderness season. My family has had COVID-19 and two of us are still ill with long Covid. Isolation has exacerbated this time of stripping away. Yet I sense God's Spirit deepening things in me and can see ways he is using this redemptively.

If you are in a similar desert season, embrace it and allow it to prepare the way in your heart.

---

[1] See also Luke 1:80 [2] Isa 40:3–5; 43:19

BIBLE IN A YEAR: **Nehemiah 7,8; Luke 8**

Luke 3:21 – 4:13

Foundational Affirmation

'O love of God, how rich and pure! / How measureless and strong! / It shall forevermore endure – / the saints' and angels' song.'[1]

Luke focuses on Jesus' baptismal experience, the foundation from which all his ministry will come. In this scene the Holy Spirit descends on Jesus in bodily form as a dove and the Father speaks a profoundly personal word to Jesus – an affirmation that Jesus needed to hear: 'You are my Son, the beloved, in you I take great delight' (v 22, paraphrased).

It is amazing that the Father speaks this directly to Jesus before he has done anything for him. In fact, Luke next tells us that Jesus then 'began his ministry' (v 23), which implies that this experience is the springboard for the many amazing things which Jesus goes on to say and do. God's love and pleasure in Jesus does not result from anything he does but is simply because Jesus is his Son. This implies that nothing can change this love and that

Jesus finds great security and identity in the closeness of this unique relationship. This intimacy and affirmation is the very thing that empowers Jesus to endure testing in the desert, faithfully to minister to people for the next three years and, ultimately, to go to the cross.

We live in a world of earned acceptance and conditional love. Yet God's love, so unlike the world's, is freely available for you. God's fatherly love is totally independent of anything you do for him. He loves you because you are his child: nothing can change that. It's not a formal love, but a passionate love, the kind of love that leads to great pleasure and delight. This love will empower you to do great things for God in your life, but these are always the result, never the cause. God's intimate love is the foundation for all else.

In silence, let God's love root and ground you. Focus on this powerful and simple truth: 'You are my child, the beloved, in you I take great delight.'

[1] Frederick Martin Lehman, 'The Love of God is Greater Far', 1917

BIBLE IN A YEAR: **Nehemiah 9,10; Psalm 78:38–72**

Luke 4:14-30

Welcoming Everyone

'I now realise how true it is that God does not show favouritism but accepts from every nation the one who fears him and does what is right.'[1]

Jesus' baptismal experience of receiving the Father's love is the foundation for his ministry, which this scene formally inaugurates. Jesus returns to his home town of Nazareth and in the synagogue he reads the key passage from Isaiah (vs 16–19).[2] This functions as Jesus' mission statement, summarising his calling. Jesus' ministry is about declaring that God's good news is for all people – and this is the foundation for Luke's universal theology and special concern for non-Jews.

Why are his synagogue hearers enraged by his message, to the point where they attempt to kill Jesus? It is not because he boldly says, 'Today this scripture is fulfilled in your hearing' (v 21), though this is an audacious and controversial claim. It is when he brings home the true implications of the universal inclusiveness of his ministry by celebrating two examples of God welcoming and blessing foreigners (the Sidonian widow and Naaman the Syrian), in direct contrast to 'many' Jews (vs 25–27). What this audience cannot tolerate is the idea that God's favour and blessings are for everyone.

This foundational sermon shows Jesus' interest in the universal welcome for all people and sets the stage for the fulfilment of this welcome in the church's ministry in Acts. It also reminds us that God is always wanting to welcome the outsider into his loving family. Who is the foreigner, the other? Who is ostracised or abandoned? These are the ones the Father is seeking.

Everyone should be welcome in the church, regardless of colour, class, social status, political affiliation, or anything else. How can you welcome an apparent 'outsider' into God's family today?

[1] Acts 10:34,35 [2] Isa 61:1,2; 58:6

BIBLE IN A YEAR: **Nehemiah 11,12; Luke 9**

Luke 4:31–44

Healing Without Injuring

'First, do no harm.'[1] Is this our attitude to others?

After escaping the crowd's threat, Jesus goes from Nazareth to Capernaum, where he has a dramatic encounter with a man possessed by a demon. Just as in Mark's account,[2] which is almost certainly Luke's source for these stories, Luke emphasises that Jesus' spiritual authority is so overwhelming that even unclean spirits recognise and dramatically witness to his divine origins. Luke adds a phrase which Mark does not have: the spirit comes out of the man 'without injuring him' (v 35).

This shows Luke's pastoral concern for the well-being of the man being healed. There is no question that he is set free by Jesus' supreme power, but Luke wants his readers to know that no harm befalls him in the process. It is hard to imagine a more relevant focus for a church that is committed to safeguarding the vulnerable and the distressed, but which is having to come to terms with the reality that it has often failed in this responsibility. It is all too easy, in prayer and pastoral ministry, to allow coercive, oppressive or damaging patterns to emerge, related to the misuse of power, but this passage reminds us that no collateral damage is allowed.

Towards the end of this section, Luke provides a hint about the source of his ability to heal without injuring. After many power healings, Jesus goes out to a solitary place at daybreak (v 42). His priority is maintaining intimacy with the Father in prayer and, though he must be exhausted, these lonely places of connection with God allow him to refocus on his calling and his true priorities. We have the privilege of ministering in Jesus' authority, by the power of the Holy Spirit, but this must honour the physical, mental, emotional and psychological well-being of those to whom we minister, or else it can be abusive.

In your place of solitary prayer, allow God to refocus your heart on his priorities for you today.

---

[1] A principle contained in the Hippocratic Oath, taken by graduating medical students throughout the world [2] Mark 1:21–28

BIBLE IN A YEAR: **Nehemiah 13; Luke 10**

An Astonishing Catch

Lord of the harvest, open our eyes to see that the fields are ripe for harvest. Give us faith to partner with you in bringing the harvest in.

Jesus now begins to assemble his ministry team. It is important that he meets these fishermen right where they are: they have seen healings and other miracles, but this miraculous catch of fish speaks their language. Luke highlights their impotence to produce such results on their own – and the incredible results of their obedience (vs 5–7): a catch so abundant that they need help to bring it in. Peter is clearly astounded, not just by Jesus' power, but by his interest in his day-to-day activities and more mundane needs (vs 8,9).

As he often does, Jesus takes this common fishing scene and amplifies its meaning. He reassures Peter and tells him that now he will 'fish for people' (v 10). At this, the fishermen immediately leave their boats on shore and follow him. Jesus has entered their world and now he is drawing them into his world –

and they are eager to follow. He has met them on their level and helped them in their work, and now he is inviting them into a different kind of work, catching a different kind of fish. Leaving their past and means of living behind to follow Jesus is a significant and costly act of discipleship.

This story prefigures the drawing in of large numbers of people through the apostolic mission. The image of the overwhelming catch, so large that the disciples can hardly reel it in, hints at the exponential growth of the church which begins a short time later.[1] This ingathering of Christ-followers continues to this day, and Luke is implicitly urging his readers to join the great missional catch of people. Sometimes God's mission feels overwhelming, and the first disciples could surely relate to this. Yet he calls us to join in, all the same.

How is God challenging you to leave everything and follow him (v 11)? What do you need to let go of to take hold of this significant calling today?

[1] Described in the book of Acts

BIBLE IN A YEAR: **Esther 1–3; Psalm 79**

Luke 5:12–16

Many Levels of Healing

I praise you today, Lord, for you are the God who 'sets the lonely in families, [and] … leads out the prisoners with singing.'[1]

Luke recounts the story of the healing of a man with leprosy, who has suffered extreme exclusion and marginalisation because of his illness. The word for leprosy points to various skin diseases which were greatly feared. I once visited a group of leprosy sufferers in Kolkata and saw people in such an advanced stage they could not feel rats gnawing at their fingers and toes while they slept in piles of rubbish. Consigned to these places, their social exclusion was heartbreaking.

This man is so isolated that he has nobody to help him and must approach Jesus alone. He does so 'with his face to the ground' (v 12), emphasising the shame and social rejection he has experienced. Jesus 'reached out his hand and touched the man' (v 13). This surprising touch is incredibly restorative after so much avoidance and fear. Jesus' dramatic 'Be clean!' (v 13) relates to all the levels of defilement and ostracism he has experienced. Jesus' cleansing restores him to full participation in society.

God's healing is never just physical. It can cleanse and restore whatever wounds we have suffered, whether relational, spiritual, emotional, mental, psychological or whatever else. Jesus understands that we are complex, holistic, interconnected people. He offers us the comprehensive remedy for whatever ails us. The Greek word for 'save' (*sozo*) captures all this; for it can mean being saved, healed, redeemed, cleansed, set free, delivered, rescued and made whole. Biblical salvation is not simply about restoring our relationship with God, but has implications for every aspect of our lives. Jesus is radically reordering society through the coming of the kingdom. This challenges exclusion and marginalisation in our day as well.

Be still. Where is God bringing healing into your life? Where do you need to ask for his restoring love? Ask him to help you bring this to others.

[1] Ps 68:6

BIBLE IN A YEAR: **Esther 4,5; Luke 11**

From Prayer to Praise

'The LORD is my strength and my song; he has become my salvation. He is my God, and I will praise him, my father's God, and I will exalt him.'[1]

Today's psalm is a prayer for deliverance from enemies who want to kill David. It has a chiastic structure in which the seven verses follow a pattern: a1-b1-c1-d-c2-b2-a2. In such a symmetrical structure, the middle verse (d) is the key: verse 4, David's declaration of trust in God, who is his help and the one who sustains him. Verse 1 is David's cry for vindication, verse 7 his statement of assurance that he will look in triumph on his enemies. Similarly, verse 3 states his situation and verse 5 is his request for God to judge his foes. The whole psalm frames and moves towards the beautiful statement about God's faithful character in verse 4.

David models a way to come to God with emotional honesty, expressing his true feelings and needs. He boldly requests that God will save him and vindicate him by his might. He acknowledges his enemies who are aggressively seeking his life and he asks God to repay evil to his enemies. He does not take it upon himself to seek vengeance, but trusts in God's justice to vindicate him and judge his enemies. There is an appeal to the spiritual principle of reaping and sowing and a confidence that those who have caused him trouble will themselves reap trouble in time.

The psalm moves from prayer to praise, a common pattern throughout the psalter. As David pours out his heart honestly to God, his spirit is lifted and he praises God, his helper, protector, friend and vindicator. This progression encapsulates much of the Christian life. As we learn to come to God in honest prayer with our troubles, worries, fears and pain, he reminds us of who he is and helps us to worship him for that reality.

How can you bring your pain and worry to God in prayer and in faith? Allow God to remind you of his character and lead you into praise.

[1] Exod 15:2, NIV, 1983

BIBLE IN A YEAR: Esther 6,7; Luke 12

Luke 5:17–26

The Faith of Friends

Lord, please free me from the traps of independence and codependence and teach me the beauty of dependence on you and healthy interdependence with others.

In contrast to the man with leprosy in the previous story, who is socially isolated, the paralysed man in this episode has many supportive friends determined to bring him before Jesus. The crowd is so thick that they must take their friend up to the roof and lower him down in front of Jesus. Houses often had flat roofs made of mud mixed with straw, so they would have been able to take apart a section large enough to do this. It is not the paralysed man's faith that impresses Jesus but the faith of his friends.

Jesus first tells him his sins are forgiven – and to underscore his authority to do this, he also heals him physically. This is a clear reference to Jesus' divinity, emphasised by the accusation of blasphemy (v 21). The onlookers are first angry at Jesus' presumption about forgiving sins and then amazed at the remarkable healing.

Jesus knows what this man truly needs and he focuses on his multifaceted needs, indifferent to the opinions of his observers.

Our faith affects others, for better or worse. Perhaps this paralysed man has lost hope and needs his friends to believe for him and bring him before Jesus. This might explain why his first need is forgiveness, rather than physical healing. The story illustrates the power of spiritual community. All of us reach points where we struggle to continue to believe and cannot bring ourselves before God's loving presence. At these times we need faithful friends around us, who can believe on our behalf and exercise their faith to bring us near to Jesus again. He stands ready to forgive and to heal, but it is encouraging to be surrounded by people who can help position us to receive all that we need.

Isolation and individualism block us from the protection and help of spiritual friendships. To whom in your life can you look for help? To whom can you offer it?

BIBLE IN A YEAR: **Esther 8–10; Luke 13**

Luke 5:27–39

Recognising our Need

'We are so inclined to cover up our poverty and ignore it that we often miss the opportunity to discover God, who dwells in it.'[1]

Jesus adds another disciple to his inner circle: Levi, also called Matthew. Levi leaves a lucrative tax-collecting business to follow Jesus; he has more to lose than most of the other disciples and leaves behind a material fortune to gain a spiritual one. What is more, he is quick to hold a banquet at his house, which many 'tax collectors and sinners' (v 30) attend. Levi wants his associates to meet this person who has transformed his life. This provides a helpful example of evangelistic hospitality for Luke's readers.

In this context, Jesus has a telling exchange with the Pharisees and experts in the Jewish Law, who ask his disciples why he is eating with such sinners. Hospitality and table fellowship were cultural norms with much bigger implications than we might recognise today. The word 'sinners' implies a social stigma of communicable ritual uncleanness, denoting unsavoury individuals living beyond the boundaries of acceptable society. The Pharisees are scandalised by Jesus' readiness to associate with people of such questionable reputation.

Jesus' response highlights his attention to people who recognise and admit their need. The Pharisees wrapped themselves in respectability, making themselves appear holy by publicly doing good deeds and pointing out the sins of others. Jesus chooses to spend time not with such self-righteous, proud people, but with people who know they are not good enough for God on their own. Jesus is not condoning sin – he insists that sinners must repent – but his ministry of restoration is for the sick, not for those who fail to realise their need for a physician.

It is hard to admit weakness in a culture prioritising strength. Yet recognising need is the gateway to receiving God's grace. Acknowledge that apart from him you can do nothing.

---

[1] Henri Nouwen, *Bread for the Journey*, HarperSanFrancisco, 1997

BIBLE IN A YEAR: **Job 1,2; Psalm 80**

Luke 6:1–11

Sabbath and Flourishing

'A life built upon Sabbath is contented because in rhythms of rest we discover our time is full of the holiness of God.'[1]

Luke's next two episodes focus on what work is permitted on the Sabbath. In neither does Luke suggest that Jesus is fundamentally questioning the institution of the Sabbath as a good gift of God to his people Israel. Rather, he is reminding his listeners of the foundational purpose of the Sabbath: to promote human flourishing. Feeding the hungry and restoring the broken are clearly aligned with this overarching purpose and Jesus claims that activity such as this should not only be permitted but advocated on the Sabbath. This assertion is scandalous to the Jewish leaders, who have become more focused on what is prohibited on this day of rest.

Views of the Sabbath understandably vary in the church today, for this debate is rooted in complicated questions about hermeneutical approaches to the Law. Jesus never discards the Sabbath: I suggest that neither should we. Yet Jesus subtly redefines Sabbath, linking it to doing good (v 9), rather than the complex prohibitions and regulations with which it had become associated. Anything that aligns with the overarching goal of helping people flourish is surely a useful aspect of Sabbath observance.

Many people wear busyness and fatigue as a badge of honour. In such a context, Sabbath practices are significantly countercultural. I have found that the disciplined observance of weekly Sabbath is an act of trust and faith, acknowledging that God holds all things together, not me. I have learned that I require a rhythm of weekly Sabbath, along with consistent sabbaticals of extended rest.

The antidote to workaholism and self-reliance is Sabbath rest. Time spent in prayer and reflection allows us to flourish. How can you incorporate this regular rhythm in your life?

---

[1] Shelly Miller, *Rhythms of Rest*, Bethany House, 2016

BIBLE IN A YEAR: **Job 3,4; Luke 14**

Luke 6:12-26

Patterns of Prayerfulness

'Work as if you were to live a hundred years, pray as if you were to die tomorrow.'[1]

A characteristic theme in Luke's Gospel is the habitual way Jesus withdraws to pray. He has already gone out to a 'solitary place' at daybreak[2] and retreated to 'lonely places' to pray.[3] Here he retires to a mountainside to spend the whole night praying to God (v 12). This is clearly a regular habit, particularly important before significant events such as the choosing of the twelve apostles, and Luke emphasises Jesus' prayerful dependence on the Father in preparation for this event.

One of the common themes of these references is solitude. This may function as an example for his followers to imitate, but Jesus is not doing it for their benefit but for his own. He needs to get away from everyone and find a place of silence alone. Luke does not tell us what happens in these times of prayer, but they are presumably about hearing from the Father, refocusing on that core relationship and clarifying how God is leading him.

When I was a teenager, I started the regular habit of silent personal retreats, first in a beautiful inner-city convent near my house in Houston. I have maintained this practice throughout my adult life, normally three times per year, before each new term starts (as I work in the academic world). A helpful analogy is a pond – when you drop a pebble in, you must wait to allow the ripples to subside before it becomes calm once again and your reflection becomes clear. Similarly, we all need regular times of retreat, solitude and silence, where we allow ourselves to become still and are then able to see with greater clarity. These have become a lifeline for me and a much-needed chance to hear again from God and realign myself with what he is saying.

Have you discovered your own regular pattern of prayer, silence, stillness and solitude? Consider scheduling a personal retreat in the next few months, to be alone in prayer with God.

[1] Benjamin Franklin, 1706-90   [2] Luke 4:42   [3] Luke 5:16

BIBLE IN A YEAR: **Job 5,6; Luke 15**

Luke 6:27–42

A Life of Grace

'When he tells us to love our enemies, he gives, along with the command, the love itself.'[1]

Corrie ten Boom somehow survived the horror of concentration and death camps during the second world war. She later came across a former SS man who had guarded her, who approached to shake her hand. This reminded her of the horrid pain she had experienced and she knew she couldn't forgive this man in her own strength. The above quote is her reflection, and her life shows the power of God's strength to forgive and love people she could not bring herself to love in her own strength.

Jesus is clear in his instruction about loving enemies and forgiveness. His main argument is simple – God calls us to be merciful because he is merciful. The extent of our ability to avoid judgement and forgive is the extent to which this will be returned to us. The image of grain measured in a basket is not about financial giving but about this kind of mercy and judgement (vs 36–38). If we are critical, we will receive criticism. If we treat others generously, graciously and compassionately, these qualities will come back to us: 'For with the measure you use, it will be measured to you' (v 38).

I've heard it said that 'Unforgiveness is like drinking poison and waiting for the other person to die'. We think it will harm the one towards whom we are bitter, but instead it only harms us. Forgiveness is a choice we must make for our own sake, before bitterness takes root and defiles many.[2] According to Jesus, we do this because we understand God's mercy to us. A revelation of grace leads to a life of forgiveness. To forgive is never to condone the wrong done, nor to overlook its damaging consequences. Nevertheless, it is the expression of discipleship to which Jesus uncompromisingly calls us.

A life of grace is a beautiful thing – and it is God's grace that enables this. Make the decision to forgive today, trusting that your heart will catch up.

[1] Corrie ten Boom, 1892–1983 [2] Heb 12:15

BIBLE IN A YEAR: **Job 7,8; Psalms 81,82**

Luke 6:43-49

Living it out

'My hope is built on nothing less / than Jesus' blood and righteousness ... On Christ, the solid Rock, I stand; / all other ground is sinking sand.'[1]

Discovering how a person gives and receives love is important, particularly when it is different for you; it gives you the chance to express your love to them in a way that they can receive and experience. The idea of individual 'love languages' is helpful for any relationship and has certainly enriched my marriage and friendships. Jesus here seems to imply that his love language is obedience. He is not impressed with flowery prayers, with people who call him 'Lord, Lord', but with people who do what he says.[2]

The image Jesus uses here is of building a house. My wife and I once had the privilege of designing and building a house and we were amazed at how much went into the foundation. What was unseen, deep under the ground, was actually the most important part, though we were least interested in it because we'd never see it. Yet it was what allowed us to continue enjoying the rest of the house for the long term, even if the outside paint ended up more pink than we intended! I rarely see that house any more but, whenever I do, I'm proud to have contributed something so enduring to that community.

It is all too easy to content ourselves with only hearing what Jesus has to say, but this is like building a house on shifting sand, with no foundation. Instead, we must hear his words and then, crucially, put them into practice. This discipline of 'living it out' is what produces the kind of deep and solid foundations in our lives which will hold us when the inevitable storms of life come. When life is calm the foundations do not matter much, but a crisis tests and reveals our foundations like nothing else.

What is the last thing God spoke to you about? Take a moment to reflect on your response. Are you putting his words into practice and speaking his love language?

[1] Edward Mote, 1834 [2] Also expressed four times in John 14:15,21-24

BIBLE IN A YEAR: **Job 9,10; Luke 16**

Psalm 55

Processing Betrayal

'...betrayal and the withholding of affection damage the roots from which love grows. Love can only survive these injuries if they are acknowledged'.[1]

The historical context of today's psalm is probably Absalom's rebellion and Ahithophel's betrayal.[2] David is pleading for God's help when threatened by a powerful conspiracy in Jerusalem, led by a former friend. In terms of structure, the prayer is framed by a plea for help (v 1) and a final confession of faith: 'as for me, I trust in you' (v 23). At the centre stands the heart of the psalm, a prayer for vengeance on his enemies (v 15). On either side of this central prayer is a 12-line stanza, each consisting of 5 lines plus 3 lines plus 4 lines. Hebrew poetry uses literary parallels and structures like this to convey deep theological truths.

David is grappling with the reality that someone he has closely trusted has now turned against him – surely one of the most painful experiences in life – nothing hurts more than a wound from a friend.

At times, a friend may need to confront, lovingly, in order to help,[3] but the kind of betrayal David is wrestling with cuts deep. You can feel his anguish throughout the psalm; the hurt caused by a friend's betrayal, someone with whom he 'once enjoyed sweet fellowship' (v 14), most clearly in verses 13, 14, 20 and 21.

Some years ago, a friend I had once trusted turned on me and used my vulnerability against me. It's an experience I have struggled deeply to come to terms with and I've often turned to this psalm for help. I relate profoundly to David's final call, to cast my cares on the Lord, for he will sustain me and will never let the righteous be shaken (v 22). If you are processing a similar betrayal, ask God to help you to conclude, with David, 'But as for me, I trust in you' (v 23).

Resolve today to be a faithful friend in times of trouble, bringing healing, acceptance and understanding to those you love.

---

[1] Brené Brown, *The Gifts of Imperfection*, Vermilion, 2020 [2] 2 Sam 15–17 [3] Prov 27:6

BIBLE IN A YEAR: **Job 11,12; Luke 17**

Just Say the Word

'Therefore I tell you, whatever you ask for in prayer, believe that you have received it, and it will be yours.'[1]

Until now, Jesus has dealt exclusively with the Jews, but here he begins to include non-Jews, a turning point in Luke's Gospel. There are many subtle social, political and cultural nuances here, with the main characters being the centurion, the Jewish elders and the centurion's servant. That a Gentile of great authority seeks help from a Jew is surprising, especially when they never actually meet. Even though, in Luke's version, Jesus never comes near the servant or meets the centurion, the servant is healed. This story emphasises one of Luke's favourite themes: the gospel that Jesus declares is not for the Jews only but for the whole world, prefiguring the coming global harvest which Acts depicts.

Centurions were in many ways the glue that held ancient Roman culture together. They commanded a cohort of legionnaires, usually closer to 80 than 100, and were well respected throughout society. They would be used to sending messengers to accomplish their wishes. This centurion has clearly heard of Jesus' healing power, has good relationships with the local Jews and is aware that he does not need to be present for his orders to be carried out.

Jesus is 'amazed' at this man's faith (v 9) and he directly contrasts his faith with that of the Jews. This functions as a subtle rebuke of the Jews and indeed of Luke's Christian readers. Jesus is astonished that a Gentile, not brought up to know the loving God of Israel, could do this. Do we recognise the authority of Jesus to bring good news to those far away, to free slaves, even to conquer death? Luke calls us to imitate the centurion's faith.

How is your faith today? Can you say with the centurion, 'Say the word' (v 7)? What limiting beliefs can you confess? Jesus, please expand our understanding of your authority.

[1] Mark 11:24

BIBLE IN A YEAR: **Job 13,14; Luke 18**

Luke 7:11–17

Hope Out of Tragedy

'May the God of hope fill you with all joy and peace as you trust in him, so that you may overflow with hope by the power of the Holy Spirit.'[1]

It is easy to miss multiple important cultural themes in today's story. This widow's situation is serious – she has lost her husband and now her 'only son' (v 12) has died, her last means of support. She is probably past the age of childbearing and therefore will not marry again. Unless a relative comes to her aid, she will be left penniless and her future will be bleak. People will try to take advantage of her, and she may be reduced to begging for food to survive. Luke emphasises how dire her situation is – she is exactly the kind of person Jesus has come to help. When Jesus sees her, Luke says, 'His heart went out to her' (v 13) – the Greek indicates an intense feeling of pity and compassion for someone.

The elaborate funeral procession is an important way to honour the dead in Jewish culture. Relatives follow the body through town, bystanders are expected to join, and hired mourners even cry aloud to draw attention to the spectacle. This explains the 'large crowd' (v 12) with the widow at this stage. Yet the throng of mourners will soon go home and she will be left destitute and alone. When Jesus tells her not to cry, he is recognising her desperate situation and reassuring her that it will be OK.

When Jesus raises her son from the dead, he makes a point of giving him back to his mother. She and her dire situation are the focus throughout. Luke is saying that Jesus notices the broken and hopeless and is moved by their plight; so much so that he brings hope out of tragedy and restores the widow's son to life. Are you in a hopeless situation, surrounded by tragedy? Jesus' heart is moved for you in just the same way.

Lord, thank you that you care for the details of our lives and that you also intervene miraculously. Replace the pain and tragedy of our lives with your hope today.

---

[1] Rom 15:13

BIBLE IN A YEAR: **Job 15–17; Psalms 83,84**

Look at the Facts

'I do believe; help me overcome my unbelief!'[1] Today, Lord, I choose to believe – and to be honest about my questions, doubts and unbelief.

John the Baptist is confused. He recognised Jesus and prepared the way for him,[2] yet he has been thrown into prison[3] and will soon be killed. This is not how things are supposed to work out for this great prophet and as a result he is now doubting whether Jesus really is the long-awaited Messiah. This is reassuring to me when I struggle with my own doubts and questions. Jesus acknowledges John's plight: 'Blessed is anyone who does not stumble [or 'is not offended/scandalised'] on account of me' (v 23). Jesus knows it's hard to keep believing when life doesn't make sense and our circumstances go in the opposite direction to all we had hoped and believed.

John asks a sensible question about Jesus' identity, and Jesus' response is extremely important. He doesn't rebuke John for his need for reassurance, but appeals to what has happened, to what his disciples have seen and heard. The proofs he mentions are observable deeds, not theories – they are the very things which the prophets of old predicted that the Messiah would do.[4] As the saying goes, the proof is in the pudding: the blind see, the lame walk, those with leprosy are cleansed, the deaf hear, the dead are raised and the poor hear the good news. These are tangible and reassuring confirmations of Jesus' identity.

God can handle our doubts and he welcomes our questions. He's not surprised when our faith wavers, especially when our circumstances do not align with our expectations. I have learned this again during the recent pandemic and found real freedom and healing in being honest with God about my pain. He has also reminded me of the tangible ways he has worked in my life over many years.

If you have questions about who Jesus is or what he expects of you, bring them honestly to God. As you face your doubts and unbelief, God will meet you.

[1] Mark 9:24 [2] Luke 3:15–18 [3] Luke 3:19,20 [4] Eg Isa 35:5,6; 61:1

BIBLE IN A YEAR: **Job 18,19; Luke 19**

Luke 7:36–50

Extravagant Forgiveness

In every moment of my life, Jesus, give me a fresh revelation of what you have done for me on the cross, of how much you have forgiven me.

In Jesus' day, dinner guests would recline on couches with their heads near the table, propped up on one elbow and stretching their feet out behind them. This position allows the 'sinful' woman (v 37) to anoint Jesus' feet easily, without approaching the table. This is an intimate and scandalous act, which quickly draws the attention of everyone at the dinner. Jesus uses the moment to make a memorable point. He draws attention to Simon, his Pharisee host, who has apparently committed several faux pas. Luke again contrasts the Pharisees with sinners – and the sinners come out ahead.[1]

Walking the dusty roads in sandals would lead to dirty feet and it was customary to wash a guest's feet. It would also be expected to anoint their head with oil and offer them a kiss of greeting. The fact that Simon fails to do this is certainly a significant cultural slight. The contrast with the woman is vivid – she washes Jesus' feet with her own tears, dries them with her hair, kisses them in greeting and anoints them with expensive perfume. Her acts of welcome and gratitude clearly move Jesus and her sins are forgiven, rather than the Pharisee's.

Luke often contrasts the actions of religious leaders, whom the reader would expect to receive Jesus' favour and blessing, with the actions of immoral people, who consistently are the focus of Jesus' gracious activity. The rationale is simple: 'whoever has been forgiven little loves little' (v 47), and vice versa. There is a direct correlation between our awareness of how much God has forgiven us and our ability to express authentic love and gratitude to him, which the woman vividly illustrates.

Lord, remind me of your extravagant forgiveness in my life. Show me what a response of extravagant love looks like – wastefully indulgent in expressing love to you.

---

[1] Cf Luke 5:29–32

BIBLE IN A YEAR: **Job 20,21; Luke 20**

Unexpected Disciples

'There is neither Jew nor Gentile, neither slave nor free, neither male nor female, for you are all one in Christ Jesus.'[1]

Today's reading focuses on the parable of the four soils, which represent four kinds of people and their responses to God's message. It is worth thinking carefully about which kind you are. Are you a 'path' person, refusing to believe God's message at all? Are you a 'rocky soil' person, eagerly believing the message but never getting around to doing anything about it? Are you a 'thorn patch' person, with no room in your life for God because of life's worries and the lure of materialism? How could you become more of a 'good soil' person, who follows Jesus no matter what and bears a harvest as a result? These are indeed challenging images to ponder.

Before telling this parable, Luke includes a surprising aside about those who are following Jesus. The twelve are with him, along with Mary Magdalene, Joanna the wife of Chuza, Susanna and 'many others' (v 3). Not only are these women travelling with the twelve, but they are supporting them out of their own means.

One of the characteristic themes of Luke's Gospel and Acts is his emphasis on the role of women in the ministry of Jesus and the early church. He wants to highlight the way Jesus lifts women up and empowers them to be partners in ministry and fellowship. In Jewish culture, women were forbidden from learning from rabbis; this was an exclusively male world. Yet here we see women depicted as part of Jesus' group of disciples, inverting social norms by travelling with him and supporting his ministry with their own money. This shows how God's kingdom not only lifts up the lowly and the marginalised but empowers them to become full participants and fellow ministers. This episode and many others in Luke and Acts remind us that everyone is invited to participate and minister in his name.

Maybe you feel excluded, or you've been told you cannot fully contribute to the church's ministry. What does this reading mean for you?

[1] Gal 3:28, TNIV

Luke 8:16-21

Welcome to the Family

'The Spirit himself testifies with our spirit that we are God's children. Now if we are children, then we are heirs – heirs of God and co-heirs with Christ.'[1]

These sayings of Jesus follow directly from the parable of the four soils and continue to focus on our response to God's message. First, there is the encouragement to live our lives in a way that makes the light of our faith visible, for God will bring all things into the light anyway. Then there is the cryptic saying about those who have being given more – and vice versa. This is a typical Jewish rabbinic saying and in this context is not about money or possessions but about spiritual understanding and revelation of God and his kingdom. Just as a muscle grows through exercise, so our spiritual insights increase through intentional use and practice, whereas they atrophy through passivity and standing still.

Jesus then makes a statement about family – those who hear God's word and put it into practice are his mother and brothers. Note first that it is not enough to hear God's word – as with the good soil and the lamp, we must implement it and do something intentional with it. This is about living a surrendered life of obedience. Second, this is not a repudiation of Jesus' biological family: we know that they are important to Jesus. It is rather an extension of his family to include his spiritual relatives, known through their yielded discipleship.

Jesus is in essence welcoming his faithful disciples into God's family. The Father leads the family, and Jesus is the elder brother. In this close relationship, Jesus loves us as he loved his mother Mary.[2] Paul often draws on this family image, emphasising the spirit of adoption which allows us to cry out, 'Abba, Father'.[3] In the ancient world, adoption was irrevocable, more permanent than biological family bonds. This invitation into Christ's family is an unchangeable, lifelong bond of affection and intimacy, a true privilege for all who call Christ Lord.

Thank you, Father, for this unconditional welcome into your loving family.

---

[1] Rom 8:16,17 [2] John 19:25-27 [3] Rom 8:14-17

BIBLE IN A YEAR: **Job 24-26; Luke 21**

Faith Amid Fear

'Let us then approach God's throne of grace with confidence, so that we may receive mercy and find grace to help us in our time of need.'[1]

Today's psalm is about trusting God amid intense fear. It begins with an urgent appeal to God for mercy and protection (vs 1,2) and ends with a word of confident assurance in God's deliverance (vs 12,13). It is divided into two halves, each composed of 2 lines plus 2 lines plus 3 lines, with a repeated central refrain in the middle of both halves. The danger David is facing is real, and he openly admits his fear (v 3).

The central refrains are the emotional and theological heart of this psalm (vs 4,10,11). In his fear, David begins with praise. This reminds us that praise is not only reserved for good times. In fact, it's absolutely essential to practise praise during hard times, keeping our focus on God rather than our circumstances. He goes on to say that he is choosing faith over fear. This does not mean he will never feel the emotion of fear but that, as he chooses to trust God, real peace will result. This same God lists our tears on his scroll (or puts our tears in his bottle) – this powerful image reminds us of God's nearness to us in pain and fear.

My family has had the opportunity to practise this psalm many times over the past 18 months. We all got COVID-19 in the first wave in the UK, and my wife was severely ill, because of a lack of oxygen and various heart complications. At times I was terrified that she might die. Both she and my son have acute long Covid and are still not recovered as I write. Multiple times I have found myself repeating the words of this psalm, choosing to praise God and trust him. Life is scary at times; danger and fear are very real.

David encourages us to be honest with God and focus on him in trials. He stores our tears, counts the hairs on our head[2] and cares deeply for us.

[1] Heb 4:16 [2] Matt 10:30

BIBLE IN A YEAR: **Job 27,28; Luke 22**

Luke 8:22–25

Where Is your Faith?

'Calm me, Lord, as you calmed the storm. / Still me, Lord, keep me from harm. / Let all the tumult within me cease. / Enfold me, Lord, in your peace.'[1]

Have you ever felt like you were going to drown? That is the disciples' fear. They are looking at the gale that is swamping their boat and they cry out, 'We're going to drown!' (v 24). The Sea of Galilee on which they are sailing is a large lake which is certainly prone to severe storms, sometimes producing waves up to six metres high. Even though the disciples are experienced fishermen, they have good reason to be afraid.

When they cry out to Jesus, he simply gets up and rebukes the wind and raging waters; the storm immediately subsides, and all becomes calm. Luke seems to imply that this is the natural and expected result of Jesus' presence and action. But then he asks them a crucial question: 'Where is your faith?' (v 25). Jesus senses here a crucial moment of training for his disciples. I don't think he's upset that they've called out to him and woken him – that is clearly the right thing to do. The problem is that they've looked at their surroundings and come to the conclusion that they are going to drown. Even though Jesus is with them, they've allowed the storms around them to set their expectations and they have given in to fear that this will end in their death.

When the storms of life surround us, it is easy to think we're at the mercy of the winds and waves. This is natural, but Jesus here is calling us to perceive something supernatural – his presence is greater than the frightening circumstances around us. He can intervene and rescue, if only we will ask. Just as Jesus calmed the waves, he can calm whatever storms you are facing today. Resist the urge to give in to fear, to be ruled by what you can see naturally around you.

Ask for eyes of faith, to see supernaturally and to understand that Jesus is with you. He will bring his amazing calm to your life.

[1] David Adam, 2000

BIBLE IN A YEAR: **Job 29,30; Luke 23**

Radical Transformation

Thank you, Lord, for your holistic *sozo* healing[1] – saving me, delivering me, making me whole, restoring and healing my life, physically, emotionally and spiritually.

This memorable story takes place in the region of the Gerasenes, a Gentile area where pigs are raised. Luke's focus is on the transformation of a man possessed by a 'legion' (see v 30) of demons. For a long time, this man has not worn clothes or lived indoors but has lived in the tombs. His affliction is so violent he has been chained hand and foot and even kept under guard, but he has broken his chains and been driven 'into solitary [uninhabited] places' (v 29). This refers to the social isolation that he is suffering as a result of the demonic influences in his life.

These demons recognise Jesus' authority and, after much pleading, Jesus allows them to enter a herd of pigs. The contrast in the man's condition is extreme – now he is sitting peacefully at Jesus' feet, dressed and in his right mind, totally cured/healed/saved (v 35). The dramatic change frightens all the people of the region, who ask Jesus to leave immediately. Although the man wants to follow Jesus, he is directed to make the miracle known in his own native territory, so he spreads the news of how much Jesus has done for him all over the town. Unlike in more Jewish areas, where Jesus often asks people to remain quiet to prevent any interference in his ministry, this man is directly encouraged to share his testimony broadly.

When Jesus touches our life, the transformation is extreme. It may not always be quite this dramatic, but the implications touch every area. Just as the man who was once consigned to lonely places like deserted tombs is now directly involved in the social fabric of his town, so Jesus' healing restores not just our bodies, but our minds, souls and even relationships.

How has Jesus transformed your life? Perhaps by freeing you from addiction, or healing of emotional pain? Maybe this is still ongoing. To whom can you tell the story today?

[1] Luke 8:35; and see note for 16 July

BIBLE IN A YEAR: **Job 31,32; Psalms 86,87**

Luke 8:40-56

Who Touched Me?

'Just one touch as he moves along, / pushed and press'd by the jostling throng, / just one touch and the weak was strong, / cured by the Healer divine.'[1]

The unnamed bleeding woman is desperate; she has bled for twelve years, with no doctor able to help her. A menstruating woman is ceremonially unclean under Jewish law, and so is any person or thing she touches.[2] This means she would have been ostracised for all these long years. Perhaps her husband has left her, or she has lost her family. She has run out of options and is covered in shame and disgrace.

When she sees Jesus, she somehow knows he can heal her. The crowd is crushing around him, so she must fight through the throng to reach him, which must be very difficult if she is not allowed to touch anyone. I picture her crawling on her hands and knees through peoples' legs to get close enough. When Jesus asks, 'Who touched me?' (v 45), it is not because he doesn't know. It is because he recognises that this woman needs to step forward and identify herself; to let her simply slip away would not accomplish the full healing she requires. Clearly terrified, she falls trembling at Jesus' feet. Jesus doesn't specifically call her out, but he allows her to identify herself, to exercise her own choice, to claim her own story. Part of her healing is in finding her voice and telling her full story to Jesus and all the onlookers.

She must have felt exposed and ashamed so many times, but Jesus is safe. He listens carefully to her, tenderly calls her 'daughter' (see v 48), is willing to associate with her and reassures her that her faith has healed her. He tells her to 'Go in peace', and this phrase taps into the Hebrew tradition of *shalom*, representing holistic wholeness and wellness in every way, the aligning of all things.

Many people are touching Jesus, yet her touch is different – it is the touch of desperate faith, the touch that receives healing. Reach out and touch Jesus in faith today.

---

[1] Birdie Bell, 1897 [2] Lev 15:19–28

BIBLE IN A YEAR: **Job 33,34; Luke 24**

Empowering Leadership

'As we look ahead into the next [21st] century, leaders will be those who empower others.'[1]

Leadership training is a popular and lucrative industry today. The world is desperate for safe and reliable leaders to follow, yet so often disappointed by their failures and shortcomings. In this passage, Jesus models healthy and effective leadership, which begins where all genuine leadership starts: with empowerment. Note that, as Jesus sends out the twelve, the very first thing he does, before even describing what they are to do, is give them power and authority (v 1). This sharing of his authority is the foundation for their ministry and the means by which they will accomplish his instructions.

After this, he gives them instructions so they will know what they are to do (v 2). His instructions relate directly to the empowerment he has just given them – they are to proclaim the kingdom of God and heal those who are ill. This dual proclamation, by both word and deed, demonstrates that the kingdom is both physical and spiritual, that his salvation relates both to the soul and the body. He then gives even more precise instructions about what they should take with them and how they should approach a new town (vs 3,4). He even tells them how to deal with setbacks and rejection (v 5), a crucial component of any empowering leader. Finally, he calls them back so he can continue to train and teach them (v 10).

The disciples have been following and observing Jesus closely. It is now their turn to step out and have a go. These same people will become the leaders of the early church, entrusted to continue Jesus' ministry, so it is crucial that they gain experience in Jesus' mission so they can continue to grow and learn.

As you influence and lead others, what aspects of Jesus' leadership pattern do you need to incorporate into your own leadership? How can you more effectively empower others?

[1] Bill Gates, b 1955

BIBLE IN A YEAR: **Job 35,36; Philippians 1**

Luke 9:10–17

Bring What You Have

'Now to him who is able to do immeasurably more than all we ask or imagine, according to his power that is at work within us, to him be glory'.[1]

The feeding of the five thousand is a familiar story – with a profound spiritual truth. Jesus is clearly concerned with the people's physical needs as well as their spiritual needs and he does not ignore the fact that the people are growing hungry. He could send them away to find food elsewhere, but instead he tells his disciples, 'You give them something to eat' (v 13). Their response focuses on their lack of food. Their measly five loaves of bread and two fish are nowhere near enough to feed this crowd of five thousand men (and presumably many more, with women and children).

With Jesus, however, the little that we have is more than enough. He takes this rather measly offering and prayerfully breaks the bread and fish while looking up to heaven in thanks to God. Then he returns them to the disciples to distribute to the people. Incredibly, everyone eats and is satisfied, leaving the disciples to collect 12 basketfuls of leftover food, much more than they originally had. The disciples' lack turns into overwhelming abundance.

I often feel God's calling is well beyond me, but this story is about Jesus' ability to multiply the little that we can offer. He calls us to the impossible, to accomplish far more than we ever could on our own. If we're not living for something impossibly beyond our own ability, our vision is too small. Like the disciples, our only response is to bring what we have – the simple gifts, experiences, personality traits and faith that we have. In Jesus' hands these things, inadequate as they may seem, are multiplied exponentially. The abundance left after this great feast speaks of his ability to do above and beyond all we could ask or imagine.

If you feel overwhelmed by God's call on your life, decide today to bring just what you have. Watch him multiply it to feed the multitudes.

---

[1] Eph 3: 20,21

BIBLE IN A YEAR: **Job 37,38; Psalm 88**

Continuously Following

'Trust in the Lord and do good; dwell in the land and enjoy safe pasture. Take delight in the Lord, and he will give you the desires of your heart.'[1]

This episode is a turning point in Jesus' ministry and his instruction to his disciples. Now that Peter has recognised Jesus as the Messiah, Jesus begins to tell them about his impending suffering, death and resurrection. This version of messiahship is very different to the conquering King, which most Jews expected. It must have been immensely confusing to these disciples, who won't fully understand this new paradigm until after the cross and resurrection. Yet Jesus quickly extends this paradigm of suffering and self-denial to his followers (v 23).

There are three important verbs in this verse, which are all commands in Greek. The first two, about self-denial and taking up one's cross, imply undefined action that could happen in various ways. The third verb, however, about following Jesus, implies continuous or ongoing action. The difference is undetectable in most English translations, yet it is blatant in the Greek. Jesus intentionally changes the third command to make it explicitly continuous and repeated.

Many people focus on the call to discipleship as a call to self-denial, stressing the willing taking up of one's cross as a metaphorical way to describe dying to one's own desires. This is certainly an important aspect of discipleship, particularly in the early days of repentance and learning about the Lordship of Christ. Yet the longer-term emphasis here is on following him continuously: this is the disciples' highest priority. This will not always mean self-denial and suffering, particularly as our desires increasingly align with his. Jesus bore the cross once and for all. His call to you is to follow him unceasingly.

Discipleship is about following Jesus day by day, moment by moment. Jesus, please show me what this means today. Help me to delight in you and your desires for me.

[1] Ps 37:3,4

BIBLE IN A YEAR: **Job 39,40; Philippians 2**

Psalm 57

Speaking to your Soul

'Why, my soul, are you downcast? Why so disturbed within me? Put your hope in God, for I will yet praise him, my Saviour and my God.'[1]

Today's psalm is thematically linked to the previous psalm, as a prayer for deliverance when threatened by enemies. It is also structurally similar to Psalm 56, composed of two balanced halves, each with seven Hebrew lines composed of three couplets and a refrain. It probably captures David's reflections while he was hiding in a cave from Saul.[2] He is facing multiple real dangers and what bothers him most is the slander, gossip and criticism surrounding him (v 4). Verbal cruelty can do just as much damage as physical abuse, and David's imagery of teeth as spears and arrows, and tongues as sharp swords, captures this. Yet he refuses to answer with hateful words, instead going to God with his problems.

David speaks of God as his refuge and of finding refuge in the shadow of his wings until the disaster has passed (v 1). This models a highly practical response to trauma and disaster. God's presence is the only safe place when life seems to be falling apart and we are wounded by the words or actions of others. This habitual practice of prayer and praise in such times is David's lifeline. It can be ours as well.

David then speaks to his own soul, calling out to his innermost being to prepare for praise (v 8). This is a common theme in the psalms, reflecting an awareness that we have the ability to intentionally influence our thoughts and emotions. David says that through his soul's worship, by using his instruments, he will awaken the dawn. Instead of spending a sleepless night worrying about what he cannot change, he uses these hours awake to find suitable expressions of praise and worship. This example shows us how to turn times of anxiety into times of meditating on God's faithfulness.

Do you talk to yourself? Do you know how to speak to your soul? This can be a transformative spiritual practice. How can you direct your soul today?

[1] Ps 43:5 [2] 1 Sam 22–24

BIBLE IN A YEAR: **Job 41,42; Philippians 3**

Luke 9:28–36

This is my Chosen Son

'I used to believe that prayer changes things, but now I know that prayer changes us and we change things.'[1]

Jesus' transfiguration on the mountain top reveals who he truly is, not merely a great prophet but God's own Son. It demonstrates his glory, in a way that leaves Peter befuddled (v 33). The voice from heaven (v 35) recalls Jesus' earlier baptism experience,[2] and the sleepy disciples (v 32) anticipate the painful Garden of Gethsemane experience.[3] Each of these pivotal moments shapes and sharpens Jesus' journey in significant ways. Most of all, this is a moment of prayer. As Jesus prays, his physical appearance is transformed, reflecting the power of this intense, transcendent experience of God's presence. Once again, it is in prayer that Jesus is reminded that he is God's Son. It is significant that Jesus needs this profound reassurance twice, once just before the start of his public ministry and his time of temptation in the wilderness and once before he starts the

long path to the cross. In these moments of prayer, his identity is reaffirmed and the path ahead is clarified. This moment parallels Jesus' baptism, yet instead of being the beloved Son, he is now the 'chosen Son' (see v 35); instead of the Father delighting in him, there is a call to the others there to 'listen to him'. These differences reflect the developing progression of Jesus' calling and ministry.

In the deep experience of embracing God's presence and being overwhelmed by it, Jesus is transformed and a glimpse of his heavenly identity is revealed. In the mystical encounter with Moses and Elijah, Jesus sees the journey he must make to Gethsemane and beyond. Most importantly, he knows afresh his core identity as God's chosen Son and all the grace and power that comes with this to navigate what lies before him.

Where do you meet God's transforming presence, knowing yourself to be a child of God and seeing clearly the journey ahead? How can you find that deeper moment of prayer?

[1] Mother Teresa, 1910–97 [2] Luke 3:21,22 [3] Luke 22:45,46

BIBLE IN A YEAR: **Proverbs 1,2; Philippians 4**

Luke 9:37–50

The Upside-Down Kingdom

'For even the Son of Man did not come to be served, but to serve, and to give his life as a ransom for many.'[1]

The disciples debate about who is the greatest among them (v 46).[2] There is a narrative irony here, in that this episode is bracketed by a story in which Jesus is exasperated by their inability to drive a demon out of a boy (vs 40,41) and another prediction of Jesus' suffering which the disciples misunderstand and ignore (vs 44,45), and a story in which they are jealous of others – 'not one of us' – who are successfully driving out demons in Jesus' name (vs 49,50). Luke arrangement of stories highlights the disciples' frivolous attempts at self-advancement. As Jesus makes clear, this behaviour is the exact opposite of true greatness.

Jesus highlights a child as an example of one who appears least but is actually greatest. In his culture, children were generally marginalised until reaching adulthood, so this claim would have caught his listeners' attention. It highlights the upside-down nature of the kingdom – people become great in God's sight as they sincerely look away from themselves to revere him and to serve others. This paradigm overturns the world's value structure: a truly great life is characterised by humble and loving service.

The child represents anyone on the fringes of society, anyone overlooked and ignored. Our care for others, particularly the helpless, the needy and the poor, is a measure of our greatness. How much concern do you show for others? So many are only interested in worldly greatness – status, wealth, power, possessions, reputation. Jesus' counter-intuitive path to greatness radically undermines this system by reminding us that the last will be first and the least will be greatest.

God, help us to see opportunities to pursue your kind of greatness. Show us how to prefer others above ourselves. Give us your heart for the disadvantaged and the marginalised.

[1] Mark 10:45 [2] See also Luke 22:24

BIBLE IN A YEAR: **Proverbs 3,4; Psalm 89**

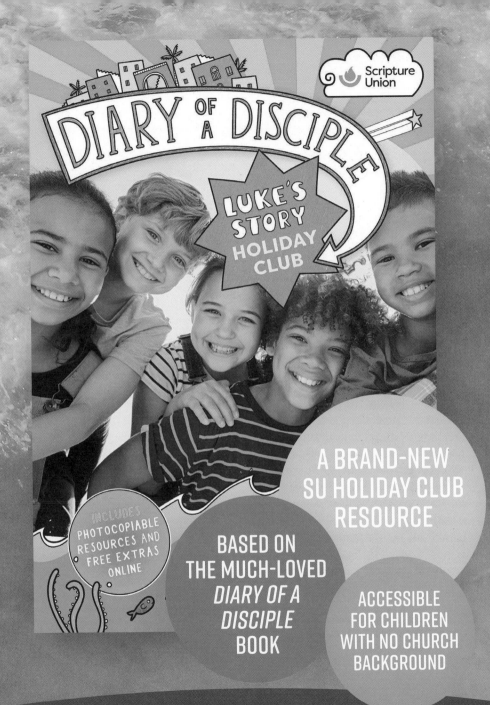

HISTORY THAT RHYMES

'In the wilderness' is the Hebrew title of Numbers, the narrative of the wilderness wanderings of the people of God as they journey towards the Promised Land. We learn some geography – probably meaningless to most of us! We learn far more about their spiritual journey, which has timeless relevance for all of us.

God's people had made it as far as Kadesh, the southern frontier of Canaan, just 11 days away from their destination, but, despite touching and tasting of the goodness of the land, fears and doubts had hardened into rebellious unbelief that kept them in a physical and spiritual wilderness for 40 years. Numbers 20–36, the last leg in this wilderness marathon, describes the *resumption* of their journey (chs 20,21), *reaffirmation* of covenant promises, albeit through an unlikely spokesperson (chs 22–24), a *rebellion* that probably wiped out the last of the Exodus generation (ch 25) and *regulations* that were to govern life in the Promised Land (chs 26–36).

To those who've recently read Exodus or earlier chapters of Numbers, this series may evoke a sense of déjà vu. The stories seem familiar, sometimes *painfully* so: murmuring against Moses, grumbling against God, water from a rock, battles and blessings, victory songs, census lists, laws about offerings, impatience and idolatry, plagues, a frustrated Moses, a wrathful God... And yet, details differ, fresh faces are spotlighted and there are twists in the tales – the command to speak to rather than strike the rock, the reversal of defeat at Hormah, the change of heart of two tribes in contrast to ten unfaithful spies. 'History doesn't repeat itself, but it does rhyme.'[1] As history unfolds, the rhyming continues. These echoes of the past have been recorded for our edification today: 'These are all warning markers – DANGER! – in our history books, written down so that we don't repeat their mistakes.'[2]

Tanya Ferdinandusz

FOR FURTHER READING

Gordon J Wenham, *Numbers*, Tyndale Old Testament Commentaries, IVP, 1981
Raymond Brown, *The Message of Numbers*, The Bible Speaks Today, IVP, 2002

[1] Attributed to Mark Twain, 1835–1910 [2] 1 Cor 10:11, *The Message*

Grace and Ungrace

'The quality of mercy is not strain'd, / it droppeth as the gentle rain from heaven'.[1] Gratefully recall ways in which you have experienced God's gentle mercy and grace.

In his book, *What's So Amazing about Grace?*, Philip Yancey coins the term 'ungrace'. Today's narrative illustrates both grace and ungrace. While still mourning his sister's death (v 1), Moses gets more grief from the disgruntled Israelites (vs 2–5). Their anxiety over the water crisis is legitimate; their childish, petulant griping is not. Moses extends grace – not turning on them in anger but turning, instead, to God (v 6).

Moses emerges from the tent of meeting armed with God's script for an enacted parable of grace – but then he fumbles his lines! All God had required was that he 'Speak to that rock before their eyes' (v 8) so that the people would witness the outpouring of God's grace like a waterfall! Moses speaks to the *people* rather than the *rock*; instead of obediently reflecting God's grace, he demonstrates 'ungrace', addressing them as 'rebels' and administering a high-handed rebuke (v 10). The quality of mercy is badly strained in this messenger of God.

Moses' upraised arm (v 11) contradicts his former submissive 'face down' (v 6) attitude before God. Shakespeare's Portia declared, 'His sceptre shows the force of temporal power ... But mercy is above this sceptred sway.'[2] Moses' staff was intended to gather the people together (v 8), but it became a prop in a show of temporal power (v 11). James counsels, 'Be quick to listen, slow to speak and slow to become angry, because human anger does not produce the righteousness that God desires.'[3] Although water gushed forth from the rock, Moses failed in his role as God's grace-dispenser.

Allow Yancey's words to challenge you: 'How is it that Christians, called to dispense the aroma of amazing grace, instead pollute the world with the noxious fumes of ungrace?'[5]

---

[1] William Shakespeare, *Merchant of Venice*, Act 4 Scene 1 [2] *Merchant of Venice*, Act 4 Scene 1 [3] James 1:19,20 [4] Philip Yancey, *Christianity Today*, Feb 1997

BIBLE IN A YEAR: **Proverbs 5,6; Colossians 1**

Numbers 21:1–9

Press On

Reflect on your faith journey in the light of Paul's words: 'I press on to take hold of that for which Christ Jesus took hold of me.'[1]

The moment was bittersweet. Nearly forty years before, right there at Hormah, the Israelites' presumptuousness had resulted in defeat at the hands of the Canaanites.[2] This time round, firmly resolved to honour God and fuelled by prayerful dependence on him, God's people savour victory (vs 2,3) of the 'first-fruits' variety, a pledge of the future conquest. Nevertheless, it's possible to win battles but lose the war! God has chosen to lead his people the long way to their destination. We see that dependence on him is replaced by impatience; battle cries turn into blasphemies (vs 4,5).

Gary Helm says this about the life of a civil-war soldier: 'Only a tiny fraction of any soldier's time was spent in front-line combat. Instead, the vast majority of his existence revolved around the monotonous routines of camp life, which presented its own set of struggles and hardships.'[3] Despite standing firm in the big battle, God's people succumb to the pressures of relatively minor matters related to route, terrain and diet (vs 4,5) – with deadly consequences (v 6). Do *you* find it easier to stay strong for one big battle rather than endure a series of smaller difficulties, disruptions or discomforts over a prolonged period? What irritations or ongoing aggravations tend to wear you down emotionally or spiritually? The upbeat tempo of 'Onward, Christian soldiers, marching as to war' requires tempering by the sobering reminder of 'the cross of Jesus going on before'.[4] The call to take up our cross is a call to *daily, disciplined* discipleship. Such discipleship is not fuelled by a series of adrenaline rushes but requires persistent pressing on. So often, the Christian life is not a brisk march but a patient plod.

Affirm, with Paul, 'Forgetting what is behind and straining towards what is ahead, I press on towards the goal to win the prize for which God has called me.'[5]

---

[1] Phil 3:12 [2] Num 14:44,45 [3] www.battlefields.org/learn/articles/life-civil-war-soldier-camp [4] Sabine Baring-Gould, 1834–1924 [5] Phil 3:13,14

BIBLE IN A YEAR: **Proverbs 7,8; Colossians 2**

Road Trip to Maturity

Consider Paul's words: 'Not that I have … already arrived at my goal, but I press on'.[1] How do you feel about where you are today in your faith journey?

When my sons were young, a trip out of town would usually begin on a high note but, as we piled on the miles, little voices would invariably turn whiny, punctuating the journey with a relentless refrain: 'Aren't we there yet?' As my boys grew older, the tone of these trips mellowed to one of quieter confidence.

Most of today's passage is a travelogue: 'The Israelites moved on … and camped … set out … and camped … in the wilderness … continued on … went from … to …' (vs 10–20). This record of their wilderness travels doesn't spell out the length of the journey nor describe the rough reality of the terrain. Yet, as they move on from place to place, setting up camp yet never able to settle down for long, there isn't even a hint of a querulous, 'Aren't we there yet?' God's people have begun to grow up!

Despite meagre details about geography, the travelogue is punctuated with poetry and narrative that record a *different* kind of journey – a journey into spiritual maturity. The people thirst, but they also trust. 'Gather the people together and I will give them water' (v 16) echoes God's earlier call, yet without the grumbling that preceded it (v 5) and accompanied, instead, by glad songs (vs 17,18). The Israelites don't simply experience God's gracious provision but also receive his powerful protection. The conquest of the kingdoms of Sihon and Og had great significance, both historically and symbolically, since these Transjordanian territories would be the first to be settled by the Israelites.[2] Their determined pressing on yields progress. There is no room for complacency, however. The unfolding story demonstrates that maturity is still a long way off!

Christian maturity is characterised by the fruit of the Spirit: love, joy, peace, forbearance, kindness, goodness, faithfulness, gentleness, self-control.[3] How does your garden grow?

---

[1] Phil 3:12 [2] Num 32:33; Gordon J Wenham, *Numbers*, Tyndale Old Testament Commentaries, IVP, 1981, p163 [3] Gal 5:22,23

BIBLE IN A YEAR: **Proverbs 9,10; Psalm 90**

Numbers 22:1–20

Hiring a Hitman

'The remarkable thing about God is that when you fear God, you fear nothing else, whereas if you do not fear God, you fear everything else.'[1]

The grapevine had been buzzing about the humiliating defeats of Sihon and Og at the hands of the Israelites (v 2). Now here were these very people, *multitudes* of them, camped out in King Balak's own backyard! Both then and now, individuals, communities and nations tend to get jittery about real or perceived threats to their security (v 3). Fear can provoke irrational reactions and *overreactions*. Almost forty years before, Israel had suffered greatly when a terrified Egyptian ruler had resorted to strategies of exploitation and extermination.[2] Moab's king turns to the spiritual underworld to hire a hitman (vs 5,6)! Today, too, nations are quick to resort to various tactics – political pressure, military might, economic sanctions, discriminatory legislation, social oppression – to fend off the slightest threat to their security or prosperity.

It could appear that Balak was simply acting as a responsible head of state, taking pre-emptive action to defend his borders. Surely, however, he was not uninformed about this people that had 'come out of Egypt' (v 5)? Israel and Moab went a long way back, tracing their ancestry to Abraham and Lot.[3] In view of this kinship, God had warned Israel, 'Do not harass the Moabites or provoke them to war, for I will not give you any part of their land.'[4] Despite Israel's military prowess, Moab's fears of invasion were groundless. Nevertheless, Balak goes on the offensive. He intends Balaam's curse to weaken the Israelites so that he could 'drive them out of the land' (v 6). God had promised Abraham, 'I will bless those who bless you, and whoever curses you I will curse'.[5] Balak arrogantly attempts to thwart this divine blessing (v 6). It was not self-defence but self-interest that prompted his actions.

As individuals, institutions, communities, or nations, how might we prevent a healthy self-preservation instinct from turning into an obsessive and unhealthy paranoia?

---

[1] Oswald Chambers [2] Exod 1:8–22 [3] Gen 19:36,37 [4] Deut 2:9 [5] Gen 12:3

BIBLE IN A YEAR: **Proverbs 11,12; Colossians 3**

Praying for Disarmament

Pray frequently and fervently 'for kings and all those in authority, that we may live peaceful and quiet lives in all godliness and holiness.'[1]

Today's psalm has three sections: *denouncement* of injustice (vs 1–5); *disarming* the unjust (vs 6–9); *delighting* in God's justice (vs 10,11). David denounces injustice in high places. The problem isn't *weak* leaders who are flawed and subject to human frailties, but *evil* leaders who wilfully misuse their position. These rulers don't just fail to prevent and punish violence but are themselves perpetrators of violence (vs 1,2). The sequence of 'heart' and 'hands' portrays premeditated evil: 'calculated ruthlessness, thought out and meted out ... with businesslike efficiency.'[2] Lord Acton famously observed that 'Power tends to corrupt and absolute power corrupts absolutely'.[3] The snake metaphor signifies that abuse of power, their 'venom' (v 4), is deadly; and it is doubly dangerous when rulers silence the voice of their own dulled conscience and grow deaf to reason, ignoring even their own counsellors (vs 4,5).

Cold-blooded evil demands a hot-blooded response! Although David's plea (vs 6–9) grates on modern sensibilities, it is *not* a bloodthirsty call for revenge but a passionate plea for disarmament that renders evil rulers impotent: let 'teeth' or 'fangs' (v 6) be removed to prevent deadly bites, let ill-intentioned 'arrows' miss their mark (v 7), let evil plans be 'stillborn' (v 8), never coming to fruition. As the unjust are disarmed, the righteous delight in justice restored (vs 10,11). On the battlefield, even soldiers on the right side cannot escape being stained by blood. So, although verse 10 doesn't advocate vindictive gloating, it does imply that God's people must fight against all that is unholy. The modern Christian's call to battle seldom involves physical attack – unlike the case of Phinehas or the Midianite war[4] – but it does involve fighting unjust structures and systems and the forces of evil.[5]

Pray for courage and strength for defenders of justice in your neighbourhood, workplace, or nation.

---

[1] 1 Tim 2:2 [2] Derek Kidner, *TOTC: Psalms 1–72*, IVP, 1973, p208 [3] Lord Acton (1834-1902) in a letter to Archbishop Mandell Creighton, 5 April 1887 [4] See notes for August 18 and 25 [5] Eph 6:10–18

BIBLE IN A YEAR: **Proverbs 13,14; Colossians 4**

Numbers 22:21–41

Good Guy? Bad Guy?

'Really to pray is to stand to attention in the presence of the King and to be prepared to take orders from him.'[1] Is this how *you* pray?

The story so far had portrayed Balak as a bad guy, but Balaam appears to be a man of integrity, committed to following God's directions. Why, since Saturday's reading ended with divine permission to proceed to Moab (v 20), does today's passage say that 'God was very angry when [Balaam] went' (v 22)? We are given several clues...

First, despite addressing God as 'LORD' (Yahweh, his covenant name), Balaam extends hospitality to those who are clearly hostile to God's covenant (vs 8,19). The apostle John warns against the kind of hospitality that gives false teachers a foothold in the community of God's people.[2] Second, Balaam makes his living by divining (v 7), something strictly forbidden by God, and is considering accepting a highly paid assignment to curse God's people (v 17)! Peter denounces this as 'the wages of wickedness'.[3]

Finally, despite receiving a clear revelation of God's will (v 12), Balaam is clearly bent on changing God's mind. Balak didn't accept Balaam's initial refusal (vs 15–17). Similarly, Balaam won't accept God's 'no' (see v 19) and so God says 'go' (v 20)! CS Lewis identified two kinds of people: 'those who say to God, "Thy will be done", and those to whom God says, in the end, "*Thy* will be done"'.[4] Balaam falls into the latter camp. Although the whole donkey episode made God's displeasure evident, Balaam demonstrated no real repentance, only offering a lame, '*If* you are displeased, I will go back' (v 34, italics added). Balaam's way is 'reckless' (v 32) and it is a recklessness driven by greed.[5]

God's permission is not necessarily God's pleasure. Do I beg God's approval for *my* desires? Or do I long to know (and do) what pleases him and furthers his purposes?

[1] Donald Coggan, 1909–2000 [2] 2 John 10,11 [3] 2 Pet 2:15
[4] CS Lewis, *The Great Divorce*, HarperCollins, 2001, p75 [5] Jude 11

BIBLE IN A YEAR: **Proverbs 15,16; 1 Thessalonians 1**

Powerful Pronouncements

'Lord, speak to me, that I may speak / in living echoes of thy tone.'[1]

God's covenant with Abraham centred on three key promises: land, nationhood, blessing.[2] It was in pursuance of this covenant that God had delivered his people from slavery, declared them his covenant people and was leading them to the Promised Land. As the Israelites camped on the plains of Moab, the threshold of the Promised Land, it seems fitting that they should hear divine pronouncements about the fulfilment of these promises (see vs 9,10,21–23). What is *unexpected* is that these oracles don't address Israel but a pagan king, and that they are not uttered by God's prophet but by a pagan *baru* (priest-diviner).

As a *baru*, Balaam was a devotee of many gods, willing to deal with *any* god if the price was right. The multiple altars (v 1) may reflect this polytheistic view. Despite his earlier admission, 'I have sinned',[3] there is no evidence of a change of heart and Balaam continues to rely on divination.[4] Bulls and rams were valuable sacrificial animals, but the offering of 42 animals – two animals at each of the seven altars, at three different sites (vs 1,14,29) – does not emit the aroma of a pleasing sacrifice, only the suspicious stench of bribery! Balaam's magnificent words of blessing do not stem from his *unwillingness* to curse God's people, only from his *inability* to do so: he is compelled ('must') to speak only as the Lord directs and 'cannot' do otherwise (vs 12,20,26).

The Lord had already used a 'dumb animal' to speak to Balaam; now he uses a greedy, manipulative soothsayer to make known his unchanging character and unshakeable purposes to a pagan king (v 18). Through the grapevine, the Israelites, too, would hear these powerful pronouncements and be strengthened for the final leg of their journey.

Spirit of truth, amid the clamour and confusion of many voices speaking many messages, help me to recognise *your* truth, regardless of who speaks it.

---

[1] Frances Havergal, 1836–79 [2] Gen 12:1–3 [3] Num 22:34 [4] Contrast Num 24:1

BIBLE IN A YEAR: **Proverbs 17,18; Psalm 91**

Numbers 24

Rebounding Curse

**'...bless – that's your job, to bless. You'll be a blessing and also get a blessing.'[1]
Ask God how he wants to use you as a channel of his blessing.**

In his first oracle, Balaam was unable to *curse* God's people;[2] in the second, he was compelled to pronounce a *blessing*.[3] In the oracles that follow, the theme of blessings and curses gathers momentum. The third oracle is a prophecy. It describes the breadth and beauty of the land God's people will soon inherit (vs 5–7a), refers to the future king who will reign over this exalted kingdom (v 7b) and concludes by echoing the Abrahamic promise: 'May those who bless you be blessed and those who curse you be cursed!' (v 9b). The far-reaching implications of this promise are elaborated on in the remaining oracles.

Despite Balak's angry dismissal of Balaam, apparently without pay (vs 10,11), God isn't done yet! Four times, Balaam 'spoke his message' (vs 15,20,21,23) of stern warnings about the certainty of judgement, emphasised by the repeated 'will', coupled with words like *crush, conquered, destroy, ruin* – against anyone who tried to thwart God's purposes. Harry Potter fans may recall that Voldemort's attempt to destroy Harry with a killing curse rebounded on himself, stripping him of his powers and, ultimately, destroying him. Attacks or curses against God's people would not just be dismal failures but would ultimately rebound on those who attempted them, with fatal consequences.

Balaam was a *seer* who clearly saw God at work and heard his message, but he failed to be a *doer* of God's word. Before returning home, Balaam had formulated a strategy for the downfall of the Israelites, not by cursing but by seducing them, to sin and thereby bring curses upon themselves.[4] Although his attempts were partly successful, for God's people did succumb to sin, God will not be thwarted and Balaam will not escape judgement.[5]

Reflect on James 1:22–27. In what ways are you failing as a doer of God's Word? What will you *do* about this?

[1] 1 Pet 3:9, *The Message* [2] Num 23:8 [3] Num 23:20 [4] Num 31:16 [5] Num 31:8

BIBLE IN A YEAR: **Proverbs 19,20; 1 Thessalonians 2**

Sin as Old as Time

'Riches I heed not, nor man's empty praise, / thou mine inheritance, now and always: / thou and thou only, first in my heart, / high King of heaven, my treasure thou art.'[1]

We last glimpsed the Israelites camped on the plains of Moab, victorious in battle, feared by the surrounding nations, poised to possess the Promised Land. However, 'there's many a slip 'twixt the cup and the lip'! Their 'slip' was a sin as old as time: the creature's failure to give the Creator his rightful place.[2] It was no accident that 'You shall have no other gods before me' was God's first commandment.[3] This command was the bedrock of the covenant relationship and the basis for promised blessing. At Sinai, even before the metaphoric ink was dry, God's people had flouted this commandment![4]

The Bible 'juxtaposes the brightest of revelations and the darkest of sins.'[5] The events in these verses have many echoes of those at Sinai.[6] At Sinai, the golden calf is worshipped; at Shittim, God's people bow before Baal, the Canaanite fertility god. At Sinai, they feast and 'indulge in revelry';[7] now they eat the 'sacrificial meal' (v 2) and 'indulge in sexual immorality' (v 1). On both occasions, the Lord's anger burns fiercely, many die by plague or execution and those who defend God's honour are highly commended. To be 'yoked' (vs 3,5) is to be bound in pursuit of a common purpose. The marrying of spiritual idolatry and sexual immorality is a recurrent theme in the Bible. Brazen sin calls for a bold response. The violent action which gives rise to God's 'covenant of peace' with Phinehas (vs 8,12) foreshadows a greater covenant of peace where the violence is directed against the Son of God himself, who makes peace in his own flesh.[8] The sin of idolatry is as old as time but also prevalent *throughout* time, assuming different forms and faces.

Graven images and golden calves may no longer captivate us, but are we captive to the lures of riches, lofty ambitions, digital delights and a host of glittering pleasures?

[1] Eleanor Hull, 1860–1935, 'Be Thou my Vision' [2] Gen 3:5 [3] Exod 20:3 [4] Exod 32 [5] Wenham, 1981, p184 [6] Exod 32:1–10,25–29 [7] Exod 32:6 [8] Eph 2:14,15

BIBLE IN A YEAR: **Proverbs 21,22; 1 Thessalonians 3**

Numbers 27:1–11

Daughters of the King

You are a daughter, you are a son, of the King of kings. Soak in the wonder of this breathtaking privilege.

Until 2013, Britain's heir to the throne was the monarch's firstborn son. Only where there were no sons did the crown pass to the eldest daughter. With changes in succession laws, however, sons and daughters now enjoy equal rights to the throne. By law and custom, only sons enjoyed inheritance rights in Israel. Since Zelophehad had no sons, his daughters challenge this practice. First, the women's actions represent a faith statement. Although the conquest is still an unrealised promise, these women act out of the assurance that it *will* take place, demonstrating that 'faith is being sure of what we hope for and certain of what we do not see'.[1] Second, they had just cause for concern, since disappearance of the family name (v 4) was frequently associated with divine judgement and 'an inheritance' in the land (v 7) was linked to fellowship with God and inclusion in the covenant. Third, although they are assertive in approaching the tabernacle (v 2), these women are not aggressive but submit their concerns to God's appointed leader. It says much for Moses' leadership that he didn't dismiss the case out of hand, citing tradition or personal opinion, but sought God's direction (v 5).[2]

God doesn't just rule in favour of these women, he declares this a law for *all* Israel (vs 8–11). Even this is only a step in the right direction. Progress is often viewed as moving with the times, but really it's about moving closer to God's original intention – in this case, going back to the beginning, where men and women were, equally, image-bearers of God and inheritors of his blessing.[3] The coming of the new Moses, Jesus, represents a giant leap forward into a new community where women would be *co-heirs* – not merely inheriting in the *absence* of sons but equally *together* with sons.[4]

Where God's Word is silent or unclear, the church must seek Spirit-shaped wisdom to make God-pleasing decisions.

---

[1] Heb 11:1, TNIV [2] See also Num 9:8; 15:32–35 [3] Gen 1:26–28 [4] Gal 3:27–29; 1 Pet 3:7

BIBLE IN A YEAR: **Proverbs 23,24; Psalms 92,93**

Baton Change

'You're blessed when you stay on course, walking steadily on the road revealed by GOD.'[1]

In a relay race, victory does not depend on the speed of a single runner but on that of all team members. Speed alone isn't enough: it's important to pass the baton correctly to the next runner and to do so within the demarcated changeover zone. Before reaching the changeover zone, there's an acceleration zone, where runners waiting to receive the baton may begin their run so that they can pick up speed in readiness to receive the baton and run the next section.

Moses was lead runner in the 40-year marathon to the Promised Land! His lap was now drawing to a close (vs 12,13). To whom would he pass the baton? It had to be someone who would be a good shepherd to God's flock (v 17). The Lord designates Joshua, a man with a 'spirit of leadership' (v 18), who had trained under Moses for nearly 40 years, serving as army general, trusted aide and a faithful and fearless ally.[2]

Moses and Joshua have not yet entered the changeover zone. The baton change would take place only when God himself confirmed Joshua's appointment, shortly before Moses' death[3] but, as Moses commissions Joshua in the presence of the priest and community, Joshua is entering the acceleration zone. The laying on of hands signifies the transfer of authority (vs 18–21). While it is still Moses' hand that grips the baton, everyone now knows that it is only a matter of time before the baton will pass. Joshua's lap will only begin with Moses' death. This transition period, when Moses and Joshua rule in a 'co-regency' type arrangement,[4] will be an opportunity to bring Joshua up to speed, ensuring a smooth baton change.

'Pass on what you heard from me ... to reliable leaders who are competent to teach others.'[5] In what ways are you preparing to *receive* the baton and *pass it on*?

[1] Ps 119:1, *The Message* [2] Exod 17:9–13; 33:11; Num 14:6–9,30 [3] Deut 31:14,23
[4] Wenham, *Numbers*, IVP, 1981, p195 [5] 2 Tim 2:2, *The Message*

BIBLE IN A YEAR: **Proverbs 25,26; 1 Thessalonians 4**

Almighty Fortress

'When you're between a rock and a hard place, it won't be a dead end – Because I am GOD, your personal God, The Holy of Israel, your Saviour.'[1]

The context of today's psalm is David's difficult in-between years – *after* being anointed by Samuel but *before* being crowned king. He didn't yet enjoy the security of a fortress for, as the superscription reveals, Saul was bent on destroying him and David wasn't even safe in his own home! Hemmed in by threats on his life, David's response is not to seek a safe house or military stronghold but to turn to a safe person. The psalm begins with a plea that *God* would be his fortress (v 1) and ends with the confident affirmation that God *is* indeed his fortress (vs 16,17).

David's life was in danger (vs 1–4). In a twice-repeated refrain, he compares his enemies to a pack of wild dogs: they growl, prowl and howl (vs 6,7,14,15)! The 'but' of verse 8 is a crucial hinge-point: 'But you laugh at them, LORD; you scoff at all those nations' (v 8).[2]

In this second section of the psalm, although threats haven't dissolved and foes remain undefeated, despair gives way to a strong note of hope. Adopting God's perspective sends David's confidence soaring: not only will enemy attacks fail, God's justice will prevail (vs 10b–13).

Times are bad when Peter, Susan, Edmund and Lucy first step into Narnia, for it is 'always winter and never Christmas'. Yet, just *hearing* that 'Aslan is on the move' inspires courage, hope and joy, even though it is still winter.[3] As the story progresses, the children observe signs that winter is melting away into spring. In our psalm, the knowledge that God is on the move, ever-present, in control and at work fuels David's determination to 'watch' expectantly (v 9) and leads to joyful and grateful confidence that God will indeed act (vs 16,17).

During the coming week, practise affirming gratefully, confidently, joyfully: 'Whatever my lot, thou hast taught me to say, "It is well, it is well with my soul!"'[4]

---

[1] Isa 43:3,4, *The Message* [2] Cf Ps 2:4 [3] CS Lewis, *Chronicles of Narnia*, HarperCollins, p118, p141
[4] H Spafford, 'When Peace Like a River', 1873

BIBLE IN A YEAR: **Proverbs 27,28; 1 Thessalonians 5**

Holy Holidays

Sing or pray: 'Take my life, and let it be / consecrated, Lord, to thee; / Take my moments and my days, / Let them flow in ceaseless praise.'[1]

In Sri Lanka we have 25 annual public holidays. I considered this a record until I discovered that Cambodia has 28! Ancient Israel had even more. The various feasts described in Numbers 28 and 29 (not counting the weekly Sabbaths) add up to a whole month of holidays! These were not just holidays, however, they were also *holy* days. The 'appointed' times for sacrificial offerings (v 2) were spiritual punctuation marks in Israel's calendar. The daily sacrifices (vs 3–8), like commas, were brief but deliberate pauses in their day, whereas the weekly Sabbaths (vs 9,10) were longer and more intentional breaks, like semi-colons! The annual feasts were decisive full stops, with all regular work coming to a grinding halt. This wasn't so workers could indulge in a lazy holiday but so worshippers could observe a holy day by holding 'a sacred assembly' (vs 18,25,26). These annual feasts were divinely *appointed*, imposing obligations on the people. They were also divine *appointments* – occasions for deeper encounters with God and opportunities to delight him with their offerings. These were not just solemn feasts but joyous 'festivals' (see vs 17,26), exclamation points to mark momentous events!

The Passover, for instance, is both 'a reminder of past salvation and a symbol of perpetual deliverance':[2] it provoked thanksgiving and hope. While pointing forwards to the ultimate Passover Lamb,[3] it also had crucial implications for the present: 'This observance will be for you like … a reminder on your forehead that this law of the LORD is to be on your lips.'[4] Not only must we reinject holiness into our holidays, we must also punctuate *each day* with pause points where we reflect on and respond to God's moment-by-moment presence in our lives.

'I'll show you how to take a real rest. Walk with me and work with me – watch how I do it. Learn the unforced rhythms of grace.'[5]

[1] Frances Havergal, 1836–79, 'Take my Life' [2] Brown, *The Message of Numbers*, IVP, 2002, p260 [3] 1 Cor 5:7 [4] Exod 13:9 [5] Matt 11:28,29, *The Message*

BIBLE IN A YEAR: **Proverbs 29,30; 2 Thessalonians 1**

Numbers 29

The Holiest Holy Day

'What can wash away my sin? ... What can make me whole again? / Nothing but the blood of Jesus.'[1] Take time for prayerful confession.

Israel's calendar had numerous holy holidays (see yesterday's note), with the seventh month boasting the lion's share: the Festival of Trumpets (vs 1–6); the Day of Atonement (vs 7–11); and the week-long Festival of Tabernacles (vs 12–38).

The seventh month began with a day to 'sound the trumpets' (v 1). Like the voice of John the Baptist calling in the wilderness, this was an insistent summons to repent. It marked the beginning of a ten-day penitential period of preparation, leading up to the holiest of all the holy days, the Day of Atonement – a little like our 40 days of Lent leading up to Easter. This festival involved the 'sin offering' of a male goat (v 11); Leviticus 16 details the rituals surrounding this atonement, which had to be made annually 'for all the sins of the Israelites'.[2] This was the only festival marked by a fast ('deny yourselves', v 7) – a reminder that even the slightest stain

of human sinfulness is an affront to God's holiness. On the fifteenth day, however, the solemn *fast* makes way for a joyous *feast*, eight days marked by an abundance of offerings as for no other feast (vs 12-38). This outpouring of offerings reflected the overflowing joy of being cleansed from their sin before the Lord.[3] When the post-exilic community celebrated this festival under Nehemiah's leadership, 'their joy was very great'.[4]

We have *all* sinned and fallen short of God's glory;[5] our sin separates us from our holy God. Atonement has been made, however, not by repeated annual offerings of animals but by the once-for-all sacrifice of Jesus, the Lamb slain for us. With the relationship restored, the only fitting response is the willing and wholehearted outpouring of the offering of our whole life!

'Take my love; my Lord, I pour / at thy feet its treasure store; / take myself, and I will be; / ever, only, all for thee.'[6]

---

[1] Robert Lowry, 1826–99 [2] Lev 16:34 [3] Lev 16:30 [4] Neh 8:17 [5] Rom 3:23
[6] Frances Havergal, 1836–79, 'Take my Life'

BIBLE IN A YEAR: **Proverbs 31; Psalm 94**

Weigh your Vows

Let this be your prayer and pledge today: 'You are my portion, Lord; I have promised to obey your words.'[1]

God's people were obliged to keep his laws, but they were not obliged to make vows. A vow was a *voluntary* promise to do (or not do) something. However, its voluntary nature didn't mean that a vow could be taken lightly or dismissed. Although a vow was not required by law, a person *was* required by law to honour any vow made (v 2). This principle applied to those who were free to act independently, without any constraints in fulfilling their vows: men (v 2) and widowed or divorced women (v 9).

Moses also deals with some exceptions to this general rule (vs 3–8,10–15), situations involving women who were under the authority of either their father or their husband (v 16). These additional provisions served as safeguards against a young girl's ignorance or recklessness. They also helped to preserve domestic harmony, since they ensured that 'neither wives nor children may substitute self-imposed religious obligations for God-given duties'.[2] Jesus himself rebuked those who were using pledges as a pretext to evade responsibilities towards their parents.[3] As in the matter of daughters inheriting, these provisions were just a starting point. The New Testament goes further. Paul emphasises the principle of *mutual* submission in relationships[4] and specifically requires 'mutual consent' for any vow to abstain from marital relations.[5]

Today's passage has three important takeaways. First, carefully count the cost *before* giving your word. Second, faithfully keep your word *even* when costly to do so. Third, in giving your word, be mindful that pledges involving your time, talents, resources, or affections affect more than just yourself and be considerate of others who are impacted by your commitments.

'Does he [God] speak and then not act? Does he promise and not fulfil?'[6] He does not! We can rely on God's Word. But can *he* rely on ours?

[1] Ps 119:57, *The Message* [2] Wenham, *Numbers*, 1981, p208 [3] Matt 15:3–9 [4] Eph 5:21 – 6:9 [5] 1 Cor 7:3–5 [6] Num 23:19

BIBLE IN A YEAR: **Ecclesiastes 1–3; 2 Thessalonians 2**

Numbers 31:1–24

God's Executioner

Think about what God says he wants: 'I want justice – oceans of it. I want fairness – rivers of it. That's what I want. That's all I want.'[1]

In modern legal systems, bringing a wrongdoer to justice involves several parties: a prosecutor brings charges against the accused; a judge decides questions of law; a jury determines questions of fact; and, for capital punishment, an executioner carries out the sentence.

Today's passage is hard and horrifying, but recognising that Israel is *not* practising vigilante justice may mitigate our feelings. God is both prosecutor and judge, Israel merely the executioner. Midian and Moab had joined forces to thwart God's purposes, first by hiring Balaam to curse God's people, then by seducing them to sin. As prosecutor, the Lord accused them of deceiving the Israelites in the Peor incident (v 16); as judge, he weighed the evidence, found them guilty and delivered his verdict: 'Treat the Midianites as enemies and kill them.'[2] Today's passage focuses on the executioner charged with carrying out this sentence (vs 2,3) and obliged to do so exactly 'as the LORD commanded' (v 7). Therefore, sparing the women is not regarded as an act of mercy but as dangerous disobedience (vs 15–18) because the Midianites might again become a 'snare' among God's people, enticing them to sin.[3] But God's *favour* towards his people is never *favouritism*. They themselves must stand before the same holy judge: later, foreign nations like Assyria and Babylon would serve as executioners of God's judgement. God reminds Israel, 'It is not because of your righteousness … that you are going in to take possession of their land; but on account of the wickedness of these nations'.[4] Even Moses was not exempt; his disobedience at Meribah had been judged[5] and God's sentence would soon be carried out (v 2).

Take to heart Peter's warning: '…don't forget, he's also a responsible Father, and won't let you get by with sloppy living.'[6]

---

[1] Amos 5:24, *The Message* [2] Num 25:17,18 [3] Exod 34:12–16 [4] Deut 9:5 [5] Num 20:12
[6] 1 Pet 1:17, *The Message*

BIBLE IN A YEAR: Ecclesiastes 4,5; 2 Thessalonians 3

Going Far Together

'No man is an island, entire of itself; every man is a piece of the continent, a part of the main.'[1]

The declaration 'God saw that it was good'[2] punctuates the creation narrative. From the very beginning, God *desires* good for us and *defines* what's truly good. When Adam and Eve made choices based on what *they* 'saw'[3] rather than on what God had *said*, things started going downhill, not just for themselves but for everyone.

When two of the tribes 'saw' that the lands of Jazer and Gilead were favourable for their livestock, they sought to stay there (vs 1–5). However, although business prospects were good, they failed to factor in God's desire that '*every* Israelite shall keep the tribal inheritance of their ancestors'.[4] In their haste to grab what seemed good for themselves, the Reubenites and Gadites lost sight of God's promise of a good land and also ignored the common good. Moses confronts their inward-focused selfishness with hard-hitting questions (vs 6,7), the hard lessons of their history (vs 8–13) and a harshly worded warning (vs 14,15). The repeated references to 'Israelites' emphasise community over individual identity and call them them back to their responsibilities. 'No man is an island', and so even *inaction* by these two tribes had the power to sow discouragement among their fellow Israelites that could ultimately reap defeat for all Israel.

Moses' timely rebuke halts the downhill slide and ensures that history is *not* repeated. The African proverb says: 'If you want to go fast, go alone. If you want to go far, go together.' The two tribes not only agree to fight alongside their fellow-Israelites but pledge to serve on the front lines (v 17) and to remain there until 'all the Israelites have received their inheritance' (v 18, TNIV). The battle to conquer self-interest was fought before the battle to possess the land.

Christ wants his church to be 'built up until we *all* reach unity in the faith ... and become mature'.[5] How do you contribute to the growth of fellow believers?

---

[1] John Donne, *The Major Works*, OUP, 2009, p344 [2] Gen 1:10,12:18,21,25 [3] Gen 3:6 [4] Num 36:7–9, italics added [5] Eph 4:12,13, italics added

BIBLE IN A YEAR: **Ecclesiastes 6,7; Psalms 95,96**

Numbers 35:6–34

Justice for All

'Righteousness and justice are the foundation of your throne; love and faithfulness go before you.'[1]

If God's holiness were a beam of brilliant white light passing through a prism, justice would be one of its brightest rays! God is a divine warrior, doing battle with enemy nations to secure justice for his people; an impartial judge, holding his own people accountable when they sin; a righteous ruler, insisting on equitable dealings among his people. God's justice is the outworking of his holiness. As the conquest draws near, God sets up economic, social and legal structures to safeguard justice in the land where he himself will dwell (v 34). So the eleven tribes must make equitable economic provision for the Levites, who receive no 'inheritance' (vs 1–5),[2] and this must be done equitably, 'in proportion to the inheritance of each tribe' (v 8).

God's commitment to justice is also reflected in the demarcation of six 'cities of refuge' for anyone accused of murder (vs 6,11).[3] Justice not only demands that wrongdoers be punished (v 31), it also requires preventing miscarriages of justice and guarding against vigilante justice. Several principles emerge. First, the presumption of innocence until guilt is proven (v 12). Second, *access* to justice, ensured by the strategic location of the cities, three on each side of the Jordan (v 14). Third, no discrimination between Israelites and foreigners (v 15). Fourth, in determining punishment, the intentions underlying the actions must be considered; hence murder is dealt with far more severely (vs 16–21) than manslaughter (vs 22–25). Finally, due process is important: the entitlement to trial before a properly constituted tribunal and the rules about admissible testimony (vs 12,24,25,30). The roots of many of our modern legal and judicial principles are found in these ancient texts.

'Injustice anywhere is a threat to justice everywhere ... Whatever affects one directly, affects all indirectly.'[4] How will you serve the cause of justice where you live, work and worship?

[1] Ps 89:14 [2] Num 26:62 [3] See also Deut 19; Josh 20
[4] Martin Luther King Jr, 1929–68, *Letter from the Birmingham Jail*

BIBLE IN A YEAR: **Ecclesiastes 8,9; 1 Timothy 1**

Our Help, our Hope

'O God, our help in ages past, / our hope for years to come, / still be our guard while troubles last, / and our eternal home.'[1] Pray for our broken world.

The 2020 pandemic shook the world. It is 2021 as I write and every part of the globe is still quaking from painful aftershocks. In these times of desperation, many fractured lives remain sunk in despair, some have loosened their grip on faith, others struggle to hold on to hope...

God's people are facing 'desperate times' (v 3). Their solid ground has been shaken and they even feel 'rejected' by God (v 1). Yet, although what once seemed firm is now fractured and fragile, a note of hope is introduced: 'But ... you have raised a banner' (v 4). After evacuating a building, following a fire or some other emergency, people gather at a designated 'assembly point' – a secure place to wait, where heads are counted to make sure everyone is safe. In desperate times, the rallying point for God's people is not a place but a person. 'Fear' of God (see v 4) signifies the people's reverence; the reference to 'those you love' (v 5) speaks of God's regard for them, because of which he reaches out in rescue.

When God's people listen as he speaks from his 'sanctuary' (v 6), this rallying point becomes a turning point. Despite earth-shaking, earth-shattering events, the heavenly throne remains unshakeable. The earth, with everything and everyone in it, belongs to God and will be dealt with according to his sovereign purposes (vs 6–8). Israel's enemies *will* be defeated – as the Amorites, Moabites and Midianites discovered when they tried to thwart God's purposes[2] – and Israel's inheritance is secure. Israel learned, often the hard way, that 'human help is worthless' and only God can give lasting victory (vs 11,12). It is a lesson that we, too, must learn.

In every choice or crisis, every opportunity or obstacle, let God be your rallying point. Allow his purposes and perspectives to inform, form and transform your vision, viewpoint and values.

---

[1] Isaac Watts, 1674–1748, 'O God our help in ages past' [2] Num 21:21–31; 24:12–19; 31:1–12

BIBLE IN A YEAR: **Ecclesiastes 10,11; 1 Timothy 2**

Numbers 36

Responsible about Rights

'Put yourself aside, and help others get ahead. Don't be obsessed with getting your own advantage ... lend a helping hand.'[1] Seek God's grace to cultivate this attitude.

In 1948, the Universal Declaration of Human Rights (UDHR) set out basic rights and freedoms universally applicable to all human beings. Fifty years later, the recognition that 'the effective enjoyment and implementation of human rights and fundamental freedoms are inextricably linked to the assumption of the duties and responsibilities implicit in those rights' gave rise to the Declaration of Human Duties and Responsibilities.

In a question relating to land rights, God had upheld the right of Zelophehad's daughters to inherit (v 2),[2] but it didn't take 50 years to recognise the necessity for the responsible exercise of this right! While 'they may marry anyone they please' (v 6), this is constrained by the requirement to 'marry within their father's tribal clan' (v 6). This would

safeguard the inheritance of *every* Israelite, a consideration so important that it is repeated three times (vs 7–9).

Paul echoes this mindset when he reminds the Corinthian church that gifts given to 'each one' must be used for the 'common good'.[3] As a consequence of Covid-19, many countries experienced lockdowns which restricted individual freedoms. Such restrictions were necessary to protect whole communities from infection. Given that the inheritance of a whole clan was at risk (vs 3,4), women who enjoyed special land rights were required to be responsible in their exercise of marriage rights. In a narrative marked by repeated acts of disobedience, the women's obedience blesses the whole community and forms a refreshing conclusion to the book of Numbers.

'...do not use your freedom to indulge the sinful nature; rather, serve one another humbly in love.'[4] How does this shape your attitudes and decisions regarding rights and responsibilities?

[1] Phil 2:3,4, *The Message* [2] See also Num 27:7 [3] 1 Cor 12:7 [4] Gal 5:13, TNIV

BIBLE IN A YEAR: **Ecclesiastes 12; 1 Timothy 3**

Scripture Union

By purchasing *Encounter with God*, you are helping to support Scripture Union's mission with children and young people. Thank you!

Subscribe to our free supporter and prayer magazine at su.org.uk/ connectingyou

HOW TO READ PROPHETIC BOOKS

The first two verses of the book of Hebrews remind us that 'God spoke to our ancestors through the prophets at many times and in various ways, but in these last days he has spoken to us by his Son'. The writer of Hebrews spends much time stressing just how great and glorious Christ is. However, in no sense is he saying that the Old Testament prophets are no longer relevant to us. I think he would have been horrified to see how little knowledge and understanding many modern Christians have of prophetic literature!

We tend to know and love a small number of positive or feel-good passages from the prophets: chapters like Isaiah 6 and 40–45, Jeremiah 31, Ezekiel 34 and 37, plus a few verses from the minor prophets; but we have little awareness of who the prophets were, when they lived and what their situation was and we have little understanding of the way in which their messages, which often could be seen as quite negative, related to the context to which they originally spoke. The author of Hebrews lived in different days, as do we, and he knew that the application of specific prophecies may not apply in the same way. However, it is interesting to see how often he, and other New Testament writers, do refer to the prophets and show how they help us to have a clearer understanding of who Jesus is. What he is saying is that we must read these books with hindsight, that is, with the knowledge of the light that the life of Jesus Christ sheds on them.

A common assumption is that the prophetic books are full of predictions about the future, so all we need do is decide whether these predictions have been fulfilled or whether we are still waiting for that to happen. However, that assumption is faulty on two counts. First, although prophets do give many predictions, these are by no means the only, or even necessarily the most significant, part of their message. Second, many of their predictions are conditional. There may be two or more different predictions as to what might happen, varying according to whether people heed the prophet's message and repent, or ignore what is said and turn away from God. If we are to take God's word seriously, we must read the very strong judgement passages like Isaiah 2–5 as

Mary Evans

well as the wonderful salvation passages like Isaiah 40–45 and not assume that all negative predictions are conditional and all positive ones are not! Of course, there is always a sense that a 'remnant' will be saved, but there is also always a sense that a proportion (and sometimes it appears to be quite a large proportion) will be excluded from the covenant by their own actions and even face total destruction.

So, who were the prophets, and what should we look out for in their writings? In the Old Testament, a prophet refers to anyone God has called to do something for him or to deliver a message from him. Their situations, personalities and tasks varied tremendously, and we must be careful not to force them into a box of our making. The 'various ways' God spoke 'through the prophets' include visions, symbolic actions, parables, illustrations, laments, hymns and personal stories, as well as straightforward teaching. However, the same God speaks to and through each one of them, so of course there is consistency in their ministries and messages.

Every prophet's first task was to ensure that he or she (several women were prophets, including Huldah,[1] the first person in the Old Testament tasked with interpreting Scripture for leaders) was 'right with God'. There were many prophets like Huldah and Nathan who did not leave writings, but there are fifteen prophetic books for us to consider. Their consistent primary calling was, both by example and teaching, to help Israel (called to be God's people) to live in right relationship with God. But they could not talk the talk without walking the walk! Look out for the many passages that speak of their own experiences, their calls,[2] their personal struggles with persecution, false prophets and nobody listening,[3] and their prayers.[4]

The prophetic books contain messages, sometimes written but mostly originally spoken. They were delivered by real people, often very different from each other, to real people, also in very different situations. Sometimes the people spoken to were individuals, sometimes groups and sometimes the whole nation. The messages might be comforting, challenging, rebuking, encouraging or

[1] 2 Kings 22 [2] Eg Isa 6; Jer 1:4–19 [3] Eg Ezek 33:30–33; Mic 2:6; Jer 23:17–22
[4] Eg Jonah 2:2–10; Hab 3; Jer 12:1–13

Mary Evans

teaching, but they always started from where the people were at and pointed them towards where God wanted them to be.

In almost all instances the prophets' main concern was how Israel should be behaving in the present rather than with exactly what was going to happen in the future! Note how often it was only with hindsight that prophecies were understood. Looking back, the way Jesus fulfils Messianic prophecies is clear, but he was definitely not what Israel was expecting! It is significant to see how often New Testament writers allude to the prophets' teaching, both directly and indirectly, but not all of it is repeated. It is taken for granted that anyone who wants to know all we can know about God will read the messages of the prophets.

One universal calling of prophets was to enable hearers or readers to have a realistic understanding of their own society and behaviour. In this context they often include historical narratives of current events. Israel's people apparently had a consistent tendency to see themselves as heroes, as goodies who

would always be looked after by God and whose enemies were always the baddies God would punish. Look out for the number of times prophets were saying, 'You think this, but actually it is you who are turning from God, disappointing God, rejecting the covenant and in no sense behaving as the people of God'. People are unlikely to repent if they do not realise they have anything to repent for, so it was vital that the prophets enabled them to be aware of their own failures.

A second universal calling, related to the first, was to tell of God's judgement against Israel and to explain clearly the reasons why such judgements were going to take place. Israel thought that if they performed all the religious obligations described in the Law then of course they would inherit all the wonderful possibilities that had been set before them. Look out for how often prophets explain that it was not just about feasts and sacrifices: in fact, God despised such activity when it did not reflect godly lives.[5]

Being in covenant relationship with a holy, loving and merciful God brought

[5] Amos 5:21

with it the responsibility to be holy, loving and merciful themselves, having, like God, a particular concern for the poor, the weak and the unsupported. Not only idolatry, but also immorality and, in particular, injustice were denials of God and his character.[6] The words used vary, some speak of punishment, others of judgement, destruction, doom or ruin, but all make the same point. Prophet after prophet announces that, because of their behaviour, God will punish Israel and disaster will befall them.

But prophets were also all very clear that although this future of destruction was a very real possibility, it wasn't the only one! Look out for how many times in their proclamations of doom they also include a call to repent. 'If' (and, sometimes said explicitly and sometimes implicitly, 'only if') Israel did repent and change their behaviour, then they could move on to the prophecies of hope of future salvation. Look out for how often these positive pronouncements come in the context not only of repentance but also of explaining that a major reason for God's intervening on Israel's behalf is not for their blessing, but so that the whole world will recognise God's power and glory.

When reading prophetic material, we must be aware of why this particular prophet spoke in this particular way, and how the readers/hearers were expected to respond. The judgement prophecies were given to stimulate repentance and renewed faith; the salvation and blessing prophecies were given to stimulate repentance and renewed faith! Brueggemann helpfully summarises the prophetic calling as 'to tell the truth in a society that lives in illusion, grieve in a society that practices denial, and express hope in a society that lives in despair'.[7] Reading the prophets as a whole, not just the bits that make us feel comfortable, can be a huge help to today's believers as we seek to carry out the same tasks. So go and reread – and don't skip the hard bits. It may occasionally be difficult, often challenging, comforting, frightening, unsettling, stimulating, inspiring, sometimes fun, but always very definitely worthwhile!

[6] Eg Amos 2:6–16; 5:11–13; 6:1–7; Hos 12; Ezek 11:1–12
[7] Walter Brueggemann, *Reality, Grief, Hope: Three Urgent Prophetic Tasks*, Eerdmans, 2014

"I DON'T GO TO CHURCH BUT..."

95% of under-18s don't go to church. **BUT** many are open to faith.

Together we can reach them!

SCAN TO JOIN **THE 95 CAMPAIGN** FOR FREE

FIND OUT MORE AT THE95.ORG.UK

FIGHTING FOR THE FAITH

Over the next couple of weeks we will dive into this letter from Paul to his younger protégé Timothy. What will become clear as we do so is that while many of the thoughts expressed to Timothy are personal in nature, they are expressed in a way to be read by the church as a whole. This letter is personal, but not private. My prayer is that God will speak to you through this preserved ancient letter. What a wonder it is that words written into the first-century culture of Ephesus, where Timothy ministered, can still shine a spotlight on our diverse contexts today.

This letter forms part of what have been labelled the 'Pastoral Letters'. Unlike his other letters, which are addressed to whole churches, Paul addressed two letters individually to Timothy, as well as one to Titus and one to Philemon. In this letter, Paul is acting not only as a pastor to Timothy, but also offering pastoral wisdom to the various congregations of which Timothy had oversight. Since first meeting Timothy at his home in Lystra,[1] Paul's relationship with him was clearly very special. While mentoring as a term is not biblically referenced, what we see exemplified in Paul and Timothy's relationship is an exemplar for contemporary Christian relationships of mutual encouragement and intentional discipleship.

There are some difficult sections in this letter. The notes that follow will not give all the answers to the host of questions you may have. As we journey through the letter, please keep in mind that Paul urges Timothy to rely and lean on the grace of God. The letter both begins (1:2) and ends (6:21) with such a plea. May that grace extended from Paul to Timothy and those within his reach be ours too. Amidst the teaching on gender roles within public worship, eligibility for leadership, relations between church and state, may we, with Paul, be preoccupied with faithfully guarding the glorious gospel and handing it on.

Jonny Libby

---

[1] Acts 16:1

1 Timothy 1:1–11

True or Different?

Father, as we come to your Word, open our eyes to gaze afresh on the glorious gospel of Christ.

Having greeted his 'son in the faith' (v 2), Paul reveals the purpose of this letter: the guarding in Ephesus of sound doctrine (v 3). Initially, Paul's focus of concern is false teachers.

How is the battle for truth going for you? I dare to say that truth as a valued commodity is at risk in our cultures, whether explicitly or subtly. Interestingly, Paul labels these teachers in Ephesus as 'false' not just because of lies they may speak, but also because of their devotion to meaningless talk, causing controversy and a drifting from the things that really matter: namely love flowing from 'a pure heart and a good conscience and a sincere faith' (v 5). Indeed, one may argue that the Greek word translated as 'false' (v 3, NIV) could be more helpfully translated as 'different' (ESV). One detects a weariness in Paul's tone as he speaks of 'myths and endless genealogies' (v 4) that pollute the truth. This is a particular challenge to teachers, in guarding against the subtleness of difference clouding the gospel message. I regretfully reflect on when I've focused on interesting ideas and theories in my teaching that, while not untrue, may distract from the glorious gospel of Christ.

Paul urges Timothy not only to defend against a departure from sound doctrine but also to guard this 'gospel concerning the glory of the blessed God' (v 11). Paul is clear to Timothy concerning the necessary good use of the Law: to reveal to sinners their desperate condition and to find grace in the glorious gospel of Christ. May we rejoice that 'we are no longer "under" the law, but that God has sent his Son to die for us and graciously put his Spirit within us in order that the righteous requirement of the law may be fulfilled in us.'[1]

Take a moment to reflect on those things that may dominate your conversations and may divert attention from the gospel of Christ.

---

[1] John Stott, *The Message of 1 Timothy & Titus*, IVP, 1996, p50

BIBLE IN A YEAR: **Song of Songs 1,2; Psalms 97,98**

A Trustworthy Saying

As we recall your goodness, Father, may praise flow in response. Amen.

I recall being on my knees at the Mercy Seat during a Salvation Army meeting as the officer recited five scriptures over me. The trustworthy saying recorded in verse 15 was the third of them. Of this verse, Spurgeon writes, 'This is one of the "little Bibles", as Luther used to call them, the gospel in a verse, the essence of the whole Bible is here.'[1] Paul is dwelling on the glorious gospel – words of gratitude and praise flow. We will encounter a further two 'trustworthy sayings' over the course of these next few days in 1 Timothy.

Having reflected on the grace and mercy of Christ that stretched deep enough to reach even the worst of sinners, is it any wonder that Paul broke out into spontaneous praise (v 17) as he magnifies the eternal, immortal, invisible and unique characteristics of God. This is an appropriate pattern for us to follow as we recall the grace and mercy extended to us. Maybe take a moment to pause and reflect on the goodness of God towards you. I wonder if there is a song of praise bursting from your lips.

The chapter ends with Paul encouraging his protégé in the battle that lies ahead. The challenge is not small for Timothy, but Paul has spelled out to him the resources he has in the God he serves. As good spiritual mentors do, Paul reminds Timothy of the promises of God previously spoken into his life (v 18). Paul is not specific about the nature of the fight ahead, but he exudes confidence in Timothy's ability to stand firm. There may be a casualty or two along the way (Hymenaeus and Alexander), but this confidence in Timothy for the fight ahead is found in the armoury of faith and a good conscience (v 19).

Lord, many of us face battles. May we, with the psalmist,[2] know ourselves equipped by you with strength.

---

[1] Charles H Spurgeon, *Evangelistic Sermons*, Marshall Morgan & Scott, 1965, p80 [2] Ps 18:39

BIBLE IN A YEAR: **Song of Songs 3,4; 1 Timothy 4**

1 Timothy 2:1–7

One and All

Father, incline our hearts to pray and learn as the Spirit leads. Amen.

Having addressed doctrine (chapter 1), Paul continues his letter by focusing on the conduct of public worship. I wonder how your intercessions typically begin. Mine often focus on that which is occupying my mind, perhaps a family concern or someone battling illness. Paul's prayer list here begins with those who exercise authority over us. What a challenge this would have been for Timothy and those under his pastoral care, given that no Christian ruler existed anywhere in the world at this point in history. While the Romans made all of their subjects pray to the emperor, the Jews were permitted to pray to their God 'on behalf' of the emperor.[1]

Paul notes that such prayer for those in authority 'pleases God our Saviour' (v 3). This is not only a statement of the uniqueness of Christ but also a challenge to any claims of divinity attributed to the emperor. Moreover, Paul re-emphasises the uniqueness of the Saviour as the 'one mediator' between God and human beings (v 5). Of this, Tom Wright notes, 'Verse 5 offers an astonishing redefinition of Jewish monotheism, with Jesus in the middle of it.'[2] Paul is not only challenging the Roman worship of Caesar but also the Jewish resistance to Jesus' divinity.

This affront to the status quo within the context of public intercessions gives us another glimpse at the wonderful claims of the glorious gospel. Paul here emphasises that 'one' God has given himself for 'all' people (vs 5,6). While debate will continue over the dichotomy of divine sovereignty and human responsibility, let us pause to rejoice in Christ who has given himself as our ransom. We were once powerless and chained up, but the price of securing our release has been met in full. Praise be to God!

Why not take a moment to pray for those in authority over us?

---

[1] Malcolm Gill, *Jesus as Mediator*, Peter Lang, 2008, p146
[2] Tom Wright, *Paul for Everyone: The Pastoral Letters*, SPCK, 2003, p21

BIBLE IN A YEAR: **Song of Songs 5,6; 1 Timothy 5**

1 Timothy 2:8-15

Stereotypes

Father, help us to read your Word today through your lens. Amen.

Kevin Giles refers to this portion of Scripture as 'the most disputed text amongst evangelicals for the past forty years'.[1] Understandably, many have accused the biblical writers of being 'patriarchal' and these verses are an example. What can we take from these verses today that will help us to hear the voice of God? Context is key, and I'm mindful that I write as a white, evangelical, Western male. Furthermore, the commentaries that many of us will read on such texts are likely to have been written by authors ethnically like me! I am aware that my comments come from this perspective and that there are voices that have been stifled in the past, of women, minority ethnic groups, etc. We cannot read Scripture without our own situations and experiences influencing our understanding of its message.

From the men, Paul desires hands to be lifted in worship and not in shows of aggression. For the women, permission to study undisturbed must be given. I've encountered verses like verse 9 used as proof-texts for dress codes within church worship settings. I'm convinced this misses the point, as Paul is more concerned with the public flaunting of wealth than with styles of clothing. Reading the entire New Testament, it is clear that women have significant roles within the early church as apostles, deacons and prophets.[2] How are these verses to be taken at first glance? I believe Paul wanted those under Timothy's charge to be freed from the cultural stereotypes of the time – let the men lift up hands in worship and let the women study without distraction. What would Paul encourage us to let go of, or pick up?

'There is neither Jew nor Gentile, neither slave nor free, neither male or female, for you are all one in Christ Jesus.'[3]

[1] Kevin Giles, *What the Bible Actually Teaches on Women*, Cascade Books, 2018, p118   [2] Rom 16; 1 Cor 11   [3] Gal 3:28, TNIV

BIBLE IN A YEAR: **Song of Songs 7,8; Psalms 99–101**

1 Timothy 3:1–7

Character Matters

Father, give me ears today to hear your voice.

I'm a fan of *The West Wing*, a fictional television series depicting the inner workings of the White House. Whenever a potential candidate is identified for a leadership role, investigations always follow to identify past scandals that may preclude an appointment. Typically, any such misdemeanour fits into one of the categories Paul details here. The more success one may enjoy, the more one's character may be subject to scrutiny. This holds too within the church, as in the arenas of politics and industry. Sadly, some high-profile contemporary Christian leaders have succumbed in areas of moral failure and perhaps neglected the fact that it is 'God's church' (v 5) under their care.

Today we find the second of Paul's 'trustworthy sayings' to Timothy. The first pertained to salvation,[1] this one to leadership. We may not readily use the word overseer in our context, but it may be understood as an 'elder' or perhaps 'bishop'. What is evident is that such a position of authority within the church is a high calling and one that should not be taken lightly. Paul details ten requirements necessary to be qualified ('above reproach') for such a task (vs 2,3). There's no mention of academic prowess, rather it is conduct and integrity that matter. Paul is more concerned with highlighting the character of, rather than the ecclesiastical duties of, the overseer.

There's a danger for those of us who are not overseers to regard this as a list representing a level of holiness required for clergy and not the ordinary Christian. While some of us may not set our hearts on the 'noble task' Paul is addressing, we are nevertheless called to set our hearts on the character and conduct emphasised.

Make it your ambition to lead a quiet life.[2] Review the conduct highlighted in today's passage and seek God for help in any area you need it.

---

[1] 1 Tim 1:15 [2] 1 Thess 4:11

BIBLE IN A YEAR: Isaiah 1,2; 1 Timothy 6

Psalm 61

Lead Me to the Rock

Lord, as we come to you, draw us deeper into your presence. Amen.

What a joy it is to know that when we feel overwhelmed we can cry out to God in the sure knowledge that he hears and responds. King David demonstrates this confidence and, as the Lord was his refuge, so he is ours. Although we are not sure of the context that draws David to record these words, we can be confident that the storms of life appear to have enveloped him.

Like David, we all long for safety and security against the crashing waves. Despite being one of the most powerful men of his time, David recognised that he needed strength from someone higher than himself. He needed a 'rock that is higher' than he (v 2), as he was unable to secure a firm footing above his own crisis. His present trust was based on past faithfulness as he declares, 'you have been my refuge' (v 3). When the storms of life come, recalling God's past faithfulness can help us see a way through and increase our faith and trust. David brings to our attention image after image of places of safety: shelter, strong tower, tabernacle/tent and the shelter of wings.

Today's psalm concludes with the Messianic glimpse towards the one to come from David's line, who will be enthroned for ever (v 7). We too must cry out to God that we may be led to the Rock. Masterminded by the Father and led by the Spirit, may we all find our shelter, refuge and strong tower in the rock, our Saviour Jesus Christ. Having begun the psalm with a desperate cry, David ends it with praise. May you, with David, know the safety that comes from the Rock who hears your cry and carries you to safety and may your praise of him be declared both daily and for ever.

Be encouraged to lift your eyes towards the Rock. In him, may you find a place of safety. Read Psalm 121 for additional reflection.

BIBLE IN A YEAR: **Isaiah 3–5; 2 Timothy 1**

1 Timothy 3:8–13

Serving the King

Lord, help me to see how passages like this can inform my life as a disciple.

Having considered those in leadership, Paul now focuses on those who serve within the church. Should we be involved in a local church, we may be familiar with the term 'deacon'. However, the role of the deacon varies considerably between one tradition and another. The Greek word *diaknos*, commonly translated as deacon, could also be translated as 'servant'. Naturally, as Christians we are all called to serve one another, but Paul is here referring to those with particular duties of service. In a similar way to how he laid out the qualifications for an overseer, Paul here lays out the prerequisites for deacons.

Stephen is perhaps the most easily recognised example of a deacon from Scripture. While not explicitly referred to as a deacon, Stephen was one of seven appointed to oversee the distribution of food for the Hellenistic widows.

While this may seem a task-related role, needing perhaps those with a flair for administration and hospitality, Luke recalls qualities more commensurate with spiritual maturity.[1] Clearly, Stephen's ministry extended beyond waiting on tables and ultimately led to his martyrdom. I wonder if the author of the letter we're currently considering paused, as he wrote, to recall the martyrdom of perhaps the first deacon, of whose execution he had approved.[2]

In closing, John Stott reminds us that the words *episkopos* (overseer) and *diakonos* (servant) were both applied to Jesus within the New Testament.[3] Peter referred to Christ as the 'Overseer of your souls'[4] and Jesus identified himself on many occasions as one who came to serve.[5] What an honour is ours to be able to share in the ministry that Christ has exemplified for us.

Consider prayerfully the core qualities described over the past two days regarding self, family, relationships, treatment of others and faith. Ask God for help in any of these areas.

---

[1] Acts 6:3–5 [2] Acts 8:1 [3] John Stott, *The Message of 1 Timothy & Titus*, IVP, 1996, p102 [4] 1 Pet 2:25 [5] Eg Mark 10:45

BIBLE IN A YEAR: Isaiah 6,7; 2 Timothy 2

1 Timothy 3:14 – 4:5

Mysteries

Father, may your word dwell in me richly today. Amen.

'The church depends on the truth for its existence; the truth depends on the church for its defence and proclamation.'[1] While not referring to a particular building, rather the body of believers, Paul emphasises 'God's household' (v 15) in terms of a pillar and foundation of truth. John Stott uses this image in describing the double responsibility of the church regarding 'truth'. First, truth is the foundation to hold it firm so as to not collapse under the weight of false teaching. Second, truth is its pillar, to lift it high so as to be visible to the world. This double responsibility is ours, too, within God's household.

Paul reminds us of the truth by quoting what was most likely an early hymn (v 16). There is speculation as to why Paul includes this hymn at this point of the letter. I think there's a clue in what immediately follows. Having held up the truth in full view, Paul returns to the issue of false teachers, instructing Timothy to stand against them. The hymn, introduced with 'the mystery from which true godliness springs' serves as the firm foundation of truth from which the censure of false teaching can flow.

The New Testament has many references to mysteries. What comes to mind when you consider a mystery? My initial thought is of Scooby Doo and his gang who have another ghostly puzzle to solve. Our ears should prick up when we hear of a mystery in the New Testament. I recall hearing a wise old preacher explain that a mystery, when quoted Scripture, is best understood as a secret that God has chosen to let us in on. What a joy is ours that he draws close enough that we can hear his voice.

'God has chosen to make known among the Gentiles the glorious riches of this mystery, which is Christ in you.'[2] Thank God for what he has made known to you.

---

[1] John Stott, *The Message of 1 Timothy & Titus*, IVP, 1996, p106 [2] Col 1:27

BIBLE IN A YEAR: **Isaiah 8,9; Psalm 102**

1 Timothy 4:6–16

Godly Wrestling

In the deeply personal words of one person to another, may we hear and apply the voice of God to our lives. Amen.

For the third trustworthy saying, Paul focuses on fitness. Having noted the importance of physical training, Paul highlights how our *spiritual* fitness is of greater value. Although he doesn't tell us what exercises he has in mind, he makes it clear that training in godliness requires us to 'labour and strive' (v 10) – terms that were synonymous with wrestling. Timothy's defence against the godlessness that was infiltrating the church was training in godliness (v 7). Pause to reflect and compare with the challenges facing the church today. Would Paul say anything different to us now?

This encouragement from Paul to his younger protégé to challenge godless myths is followed by an endorsement of Timothy's ministry. Paul affirms Timothy as gifted of God (v 14), despite his youthfulness. I've observed this as a challenge to young leaders who may be ministering among people twice their age. To the young, Paul says don't let others look down on you because of your age; while not explicitly stated here, I'm sure he'd warn older people not to do this.

These verses conclude with what Tom Wright notes as 'the instruction clergy find it hardest to hear'.[1] As a lay worker in Christian ministry, I can testify that the need for this instruction, to 'Keep a close watch on yourself' (v 16, ESV), is not restricted to clergy. This may be a salutary word for all of us as we consider who we are becoming. How is your spiritual fitness progressing? I previously worked in banking and recall being trained on identifying forged bank notes. We were trained by studying in great detail genuine notes, so it was easy to spot a fake. Look at the things Timothy is urged to devote himself to. I suspect myths and old wives' tales were easy for him to spot.

Is there a gift you have that lies dormant? Lord, grant us courage. Amen.

[1] Tom Wright, *Paul for Everyone: The Pastoral Letters*, SPCK, 2003, p52

BIBLE IN A YEAR: Isaiah 10–12; 2 Timothy 3

The Lowest and Least

'A father to the fatherless, a defender of widows, is God in his holy dwelling.'[1]

Sometimes the chapter breaks in the Bible can be unhelpful. Paul continues to address Timothy's youthful leadership as he instructs on appropriate conduct in the church family. John Stott's advice to those given responsibility beyond their years is that sensitivity to different age ranges will lead to others gratefully receiving your ministry.[2] The guidelines to Timothy for leading the church community come with warnings. The dangers of the misappropriation of power (v 1), sex (v 2) and money (v 8) undergird this teaching. Little has changed.

What follows are detailed instructions on the provision for widows, who at that time would likely have been the neediest group. This would particularly have been so for those who had become Christians, as they might well have been disowned by their families. In a world without the provision of state social welfare, it is easy to see how a Christian widow would be so vulnerable. Paul writes as one who had significant experience in helping the early church to organise community life. His specific advice is fascinating and I'd encourage you to consult a commentary to learn about the world in which he lived.

The issue in your particular community may not be the provision for widows, but I wonder who the 'least and the lowest' are within your reach? This is a challenge for the church of the twenty-first century. Paul is clear that it is a fundamental Christian duty to provide for our relatives (v 8), but should there be those who lack such support then the church needs to step up. Paul is renowned for his doctrinal prowess, but his attention to social responsibility could be easily overlooked. In this letter we see how the gospel message should spill over into social outreach. May we respond accordingly.

What does the Lord require of you? Micah 6:8 may help.

---

[1] Ps 68:5 [2] John Stott, *The Message of 1 Timothy & Titus*, IVP, 1996, p126

BIBLE IN A YEAR: **Isaiah 13,14; 2 Timothy 4**

Double Honour

Lord, as I read your word, help me to allow it to read my heart. Amen.

I wonder if during the writing of an email you've come to the point of thinking 'I mustn't forget to mention x or y'. Then, the 'cut and paste' facility in word processing is very useful in rearranging things into a coherent order. Often, I reorder my prose in email correspondence like this and, as I read this section of the letter, it is as if Paul had a few additional things on his mind to record. What we mustn't lose, among quick-fire references to 'elect angels' (v 21) and 'wine because of your stomach' (v 23), is the need for honour towards those appointed to shepherd the sheep.

While I was researching for today's notes, my wife interrupted me and asked what my hourly rate of pay was. I didn't know the answer and will curiously pick up the conversation later. Most biblical translations of the text speak of 'double honour' (v 17) and it is quite clear that Paul is referring here to financial remuneration. While not directly linked by Paul, what a travesty it would be for an elder in the church to be unable to fulfil the earlier charge to provide for his family (v 8). Sadly, I've come across many gifted church leaders who have left full-time ministry for other work so they can more adequately provide for their family.

However, honour for leaders within the church mustn't be limited to financial reward. Unfair accusations (v 19) can be crippling to those in leadership; gifted leaders have fallen as a result. This is not to minimise the need for accountability when an accusation may be justified: discernment is necessary in dealing with discipline within our churches. Is it any wonder, when addressing such issues, that Paul implores Timothy a second time to keep himself pure (v 22)?

Take a moment to pray for those who are in leadership within your church community.

What Enslaves You?

Lord, break our hearts today with the things that break yours. Amen.

Verses 6–10 are a strong indictment of modern Western culture. There has never been a time of so much wealth in the world. At the time of writing, the richest 1 per cent of people own 43 per cent of the world's wealth but 9 per cent (690 million people) will go to bed tonight hungry.[1] These shocking statistics show how things have gone wrong. There are sufficient resources in the world for us all, but the rich get richer while the poor continue to suffer. Paul says, 'the love of money is a root of all kinds of evil' (v 10). It is too simplistic to attribute world poverty to a minority's desire for wealth, yet our cravings for more for ourselves can lead to less for others.

Verse 10 is often misquoted, omitting 'the love of', and consequently wealth is viewed as evil. Paul is not opposed to wealth but is highlighting the battle between contentment and covetousness.

Anything that we covet has the danger of becoming an idol to us. To many, the idol is money, but 'the love of' anything that takes our gaze away from Christ must be guarded against.

How is this battle between covetousness and contentment going for you? I've sat both at banquet tables with the wealthy and in slum gutters with the destitute and have often observed a more genuine contentment in the gutter. Nevertheless, the church is called to help people out of the gutter. Paul is saying that there is a different way that the church should model. Luther famously wrote, 'I have held many things in my hands, and I have lost them all; but whatever I have placed in God's hands, that I still possess.'[2] May we be granted the wisdom to know what to hold loosely and what to tighten our grip on.

Father, highlight those things that take our gaze off you and give us the courage to look away.

[1] https://inequality.org/facts/global-inequality [2] Ray Comfort, *Luther Gold*, Bridge-Logos (US), 2009, p50

BIBLE IN A YEAR: Isaiah 17–20; Titus 1

Psalm 62

Refuge over Riches

Lord, give us a glimpse today of the inheritance that is ours in you. Amen.

David begins many of his psalms by telling of his great need, accompanied by a description of a very present crisis. As such psalms progress, we witness his faith rise as he recalls God's faithfulness and reliance on his current care. Psalm 62 bucks the trend. Clearly in a time of trouble, David commences with a declaration of his confidence in God. I recall a preacher referring to a particular verse of Scripture as one to brush your teeth with each morning. How about making the opening couple of verses of this psalm a declaration to begin your day?

David names some of the challenges he faces, but he asks God for nothing. This psalm oozes faith and trust and is devoid of despair, fear or petition. As in the previous psalm, David emphasises where he finds refuge. I find it captivating how David personalises the characteristics of God in the sure confidence that they are his. Spurgeon notes, 'Observe how the psalmist brands his own initials upon every name which he rejoicingly gives to his God – *my* rock, *my* salvation, *my* fortress.'[1] Wonderfully, having applied God's nature to his own context, David widens the reach of God to us all. God is '*my* refuge' (see v 7) shifts to 'God is *our* refuge' (see v 8) and David's initials are substituted with yours and mine.

Having laid claim to where to put one's trust, the psalm closes with emphasis on the futility of placing it elsewhere. As one of much wealth, King David recognises the fleeting nature of riches, described by Spurgeon as 'only so much as foam of the sea'. The foam of the sea will disappear while your gaze is still upon it, but in Christ you have an inheritance that is yours now and cannot be taken away.

Maybe take a moment today to pause and give thanks for the treasure you have in Christ.

---

[1] Charles H Spurgeon (Alister McGrath and J I Packer, eds), *Psalms (Vol 1)*, Crossway, 1993, p253

BIBLE IN A YEAR: **Isaiah 21,22; Titus 2**

What are you Pursuing?

As we come to God's Word today, may we be reminded where our treasure lies.

Paul indicates what it is necessary to pursue (v 11) in the fight between covetousness and contentment. The list has echoes of his plea to the believers in Ephesus to 'live a life worthy of the calling you have received'.[1] What is apparent is that these weapons for the good fight of faith are very different from the destructive ones of a typical battle. Having rejoiced in the hope of eternal life on confession of Christ as Lord, Paul breaks out into praise (vs 15,16). It is as if the wonder of the glorious gospel prompts continual praise from Paul.

Having acknowledged the majesty of God, Paul reiterates the theme concerning wealth. Paul's advice for the rich is to use their wealth for good, which is a noteworthy contrast to the command of Jesus to the rich young ruler to give all his wealth away at once.[2] There is much to ponder here as we consider the commands of Scripture. For the rich young ruler his wealth had clearly become his idol and needed to be cut off completely, yet here we observe a plea for generosity and sharing, rather than a laying down.

Paul closes the letter by personally addressing Timothy (v 20) in a manner that some feel he'd have written himself rather than dictating to a scribe. Nonetheless, the grace Paul extends in closing is addressed to all. The 'you' is plural, indicating that throughout the letter Paul has been looking beyond Timothy to the believers he served. Wonderfully, this letter has been preserved and that grace has been extended to us as well. The letter began with an extension of grace[3] and so it ends. In all of the warnings, encouragements and instructions which have filled the letter, may we too know ourselves enveloped by the grace of God that is offered to all.

'For where your treasure is, there your heart will be also.'[4]

[1] Eph 4:1,2 [2] Luke 18:18–30 [3] 1 Tim 1:2 [4] Matt 6:21

BIBLE IN A YEAR: **Isaiah 23,24; Titus 3**

2 Samuel 10–24

DAVID:
A HERO WITH FLAWS

The book of 2 Samuel records Israel's history during David's reign. This section records a series of incidents in the latter section of that reign, concentrating largely but not exclusively on David's leadership. However, they are not just accurate accounts of past events. Like all Scripture, these stories are 'God-breathed and ... useful for teaching, rebuking, correcting and training in righteousness'.[1] We should read the chapters not just observing what happened, but also asking what we are meant to be learning and why, given the inevitable limitations on space, the author has chosen to include these particular stories. Each day we can only concentrate on a few verses, but the account is not just a collection of individual stories but a carefully composed book. We should therefore be looking out for ongoing concerns and interests that arise, asking what this very gifted author is intending us to learn, how he expects us to feel and what difference it might make to the way we live our lives for God.

The chapters convey a real sense of affection and appreciation of David, but there seems to be a special concern for pointing out his weaknesses and failures. It is possible that the writer is reflecting on 1 Samuel 13:14 and asking whether David really was the one God sought, who was 'after his own heart'. David as psalmist fits this picture well, but the stories we shall read do raise doubts about David as king! Look out, too, for the way David interacts with others, his attitude to keeping promises, his treatment of his family, his close but strained relationship with Joab – and maybe for other ongoing themes not mentioned here.

Mary Evans

[1] 2 Tim 3:16 [2] Acts 13:22

Spiralling out of Control

'The Lord is my strength and my shield; my heart trusts in him, and he helps me. My heart leaps for joy, and with my song I praise him.'[1]

The opening phrase, 'In the course of time', reminds us that we don't have a detailed account of all that happened, just a selection of events and actions that writers saw as significant. Our challenge is to work out what is significant about each situation that is recorded and what we might learn from it! The actual events here are clear, and we have seen many such events repeated throughout history and particularly in recent years. Often, the circumstances are international, but the pattern is also seen in national, regional, family and even church contexts. Two leaders had a good relationship. One attempts to continue that relationship with the succeeding regime, but the trust, essential for such links, has, for some unknown reason, completely disappeared. Lack of trust leads to proactive aggression, which leads to full-blown war, which leads to other nations entering the fray, leading to the deaths of many thousands.

Interestingly, here it is Aram and Ammon who come off worst in the end.

So, should we concentrate on the need to assume that people can be trusted until they actually prove untrustworthy, or maybe on the importance of leaders going themselves and not just sending a delegation? Or should our focus be the need to identify and support those in our service who have been mistreated? Must we assume all aggression should automatically evoke strong and violent response? Is the writer's main concern to point out that Joab and not David was leading the army and to emphasise Joab's skill as an army commander? This is a detailed and complex account, with many possible lessons – we must be asking ourselves which one is particularly being drawn to our attention when we read this story carefully ourselves.

Lord, please help us to avoid actions which are likely to cause responses that can then spiral out of control.

[1] Ps 28:7

BIBLE IN A YEAR: Isaiah 25,26; Psalm 104

2 Samuel 11

Actions and Reactions

'Fight the good fight with all thy might! / Christ is thy strength, and Christ thy right; / lay hold on life, and it shall be / thy joy and crown eternally.'[1]

A primary task for Israel's king was to lead the army. Saul was called to fight the Philistines.[2] For David, the enemy was different but there is no indication that this task had been removed. The writer's implicit criticism of David in 2 Samuel 10:7 is made explicit here. There seems no doubt that verse 1 deliberately makes that point. David was apparently abdicating his responsibilities. The criticism of David in this chapter is clear and severe. We know that he later repented, but the story as written does not allow readers to escape the inference that his reputation as a great king was, at this point, totally unjustified. Afternoon rest was normal, but it was evening (v 2) before David got up from his bed! He had clearly not sent Joab off to war because he was concentrating on other kingly tasks! We again see spiralling consequences. His lust leads to adultery, which, given the imbalance in their status, was probably, in effect, rape. When Bathsheba became pregnant, he tried to avoid responsibility by deceiving, cheating and eventually murdering an honourable and innocent man. At the same time, he made himself vulnerable to undue influence, if not blackmail, from Joab! No wonder the thing, or indeed things, 'David had done displeased the LORD' (v 27).

Too often we have seen instances, both in nations and sadly also in churches, where popular, charismatic leaders, particularly if they claim to support our own political stance or religious preferences, are allowed to avoid responsibility for serious behavioural failures. Scripture here does not permit us to take up that position. We will need to read on to see if this chapter presents an aberration or a norm for David's fulfilling of his kingly role!

Discuss with a friend whether our tendency to view biblical characters as heroes might lead us to underestimate criticisms in the text. Might this influence how we critique modern leaders?

[1] JSB Monsell, 1863 [2] 1 Sam 9:16

BIBLE IN A YEAR: Isaiah 27,28; Philemon 1

Inevitable Consequences

'How priceless is your unfailing love, O God! People take refuge in the shadow of your wings.'[1]

We have probably all encountered situations where minds are changed and actions taken because someone is persuaded that it was their own idea! Nathan's brilliant story causes David to condemn his own behaviour! Perhaps even the pet lamb picture made David remember his own youth. He recognised that the story represented a real situation and he was shocked and furious. A man who had abundant wealth, including many sheep, felt so entitled that he took and killed a poor man's pet lamb. If the poor man was a bonded tenant, that would in theory have been legal, but there was no doubt it was a horrific misuse of privilege.

David clearly had many deficiencies as a king, but his anger here does indicate his basic decency as a human being! He knew instinctively that anyone who behaved in such a contemptible and mean way deserved the strongest condemnation and punishment. Imagine his horror when he realised that the story was about himself. He had been given so much (v 8) yet his behaviour not only ignored or even despised God's word, but despised God himself by acting as if God's many gifts to him were not enough (v 9). He had sinned not only against Bathsheba and Uriah, but against God. Nathan makes it clear that there would be both short-term and long-term consequences. Prophecies like this are not necessarily suggesting that God will deliberately cause David's own family to offend against him, but that David's behaviour provides them with an example and an excuse.

Jesus' story of the lost son[2] picks up on the message of verses 13 and 14: the prodigal can be forgiven and welcomed, but consequences remain. The prodigal will not regain the inheritance he has wasted: everything now belongs to his older brother.

Lord, if my sense of entitlement ever causes the deprivation of others, please help me to recognise what has happened and take what action I can to put it right.

---

[1] Ps 36:7 [2] Luke 15:11–32

BIBLE IN A YEAR: **Isaiah 29,30; Hebrews 1**

2 Samuel 12:15–31

Hoping and Moving On

'For with you is the fountain of life; in your light we see light.'[1]

Have you ever found yourself puzzled, or even shocked, by the behaviour or perspective of someone from another culture? I remember someone commenting on how rude people from a particular south Asian culture were because they didn't say thank you when they were served in a shop. It was a revelation to me as a British person when I was told that constantly to thank someone for doing their job was seen as implying that you had expected them not to do it right. This passage raises the same kind of issues. David's colleagues were as bewildered as modern readers by what was going on but for different reasons. They had no problem in grasping why the baby should die, but David's pleading with God while the baby lived and yet apparently easily moving on when he died, was incomprehensible! The writer wants us to grasp David's understanding of God's character.

David's desperate prayer, followed by his calm acceptance, showed that he understood that God was living and active; he could and did respond to human prayer and was able (v 13) to show undeserved mercy. David also understood that God was free to act as he thought best. David's prayer was not an attempt to blackmail God into doing what David wanted, but rather an honest expression of his own feelings, while also seeking out God's will in this situation. Once the baby died, it was clear that no other way was possible, so prayer and fasting were no longer appropriate. Sometimes it is right to keep on praying[2] and sometimes it is right to accept the inevitable and move on.[3] David understood that and, although there is nothing about his behaviour in chapter 11 to commend, here he does provide us with an example to follow.

Lord God, help us to trust in your love and your sovereignty, even when our desperate praying seems to have been disregarded and we really don't understand.

---

[1] Ps 36:9 [2] Luke 18:1–8 [3] 2 Cor 12:8–10

BIBLE IN A YEAR: **Isaiah 31,32; Psalm 105**

Entitled to Abuse?

'...he was pierced for our transgressions, he was crushed for our iniquities; the punishment that brought us peace was on him, and by his wounds we are healed.'[1]

We constantly see accounts of appalling abuse of many kinds. 'Man's inhumanity to man'[2] has not changed much over the centuries! It is hard to see how anyone could read this passage and not be horrified. Two privileged young cousins conspire together to plan an assault on an innocent and defenceless woman. They knew that what they planned was wrong, but they saw any effect their plan might have on Tamar as irrelevant. All that mattered was the fulfilment of Amnon's desire. What he wanted he had to have, whether that involved raping Tamar or throwing her out into the street. The writer wants readers to be horrified. Note the words describing Amnon: he 'fell in love', 'became so obsessed', 'grabbed', 'raped', 'hated', 'with intense hatred' (vs 1,2,11,14,15). Note, also, the way in which the writer speaks of Tamar; her thoughts and feelings are made clear. She was not recognised as a person by the two conspirators, but she was by the writer: as in the poignant description of the way such a lovely, generous girl, became a 'desolate woman' (v 20), her clothes torn and ruined, just as she had been. There is no way this passage could be interpreted as God approving of such awful abuse.

So why are we told this story in this way? David's involvement seems marginal, but although in that context Tamar going to visit Amnon would be seen as inappropriate, David finds it impossible to deny his son anything. Although he was 'furious' (v 21), his failure to either punish his son or support his daughter is significant. Amnon was following his father's example: he wanted so he took. The after-effects of David's sin continue.

The danger of concentrating on our own wants, while seeing other people as irrelevant, is not restricted to horrific situations like this. Lord, keep me from that sin.

[1] Isa 53:5 [2] Robert Burns, 'Man was Made to Mourn: A Dirge', 1784

BIBLE IN A YEAR: **Isaiah 33,34; Hebrews 2**

Psalm 63

A God Worth Serving

'God of grace and God of glory, / on your people pour your power ... Grant us wisdom, grant us courage, / for the facing of this hour.'[1]

This is one of the great psalms where David reflects on his own situation and on his knowledge of God, moving from present to past and on to the future. Unlike historical books, the main point of psalms for readers is not necessarily what they tell about the writer's life. It is rather that they give words to express our own feelings in all kinds of circumstances. Here the circumstance is living away from society in a desert, hiding from dangerous enemies. It may not be where you are now, but many of us have felt isolation, deprivation and fear like this, and we are all likely to know people still in that situation. It is wonderful to be able to point them to psalms like this, as well as to great triumphant psalms that express our feelings in 'up' times but can be less helpful when we are 'down'.

The psalmist, in the desert, longs for water and longs to experience God. The implication is that just now he can't find either. It is so helpful to know it is OK to tell God we feel like that! David looks back to times when he was 'in the sanctuary' (v 2), feeling close to God, and reminds himself both of what he knew about God then and of the reality of the commitment that he had made to trust God. His circumstances had changed, but God had not: he was still more fulfilling than rich food (v 5)! David lies awake at night, but thinking of God, and remembering past help given, help him move forward. There are psalms where the psalmist can only manage to ask 'how long?'[2] but here he is confident that, eventually, his enemies will get their comeuppance and he will be able to rejoice again.

Lord, when I feel alone and desperate, help me to remember that you are 'my God' (v 1); when I 'cling to you; your right hand upholds me' (v 8).

[1] HE Fosdick, 1930 [2] Eg Pss 13,35

BIBLE IN A YEAR: **Isaiah 35,36; Hebrews 3**

2 Samuel 13:23–39

Inevitable Consequences?

'Peace I leave ... my peace I give ... I do not give ... as the world gives. Do not let your hearts be troubled and do not be afraid.'[1]

It doesn't take much imagination to work out what happened next. Absalom, Tamar's full brother, waited two years before he took his revenge, maybe waiting to see if David really would let Amnon get away with it. He probably saw Amnon's murder as a legitimate exercise of justice. The similarity of his plan to that of Amnon and Jonadab is probably not coincidental. David suspected that Absalom's invitation was not without ulterior motives, although his unwillingness to challenge his sons may have left him with the hope that Absalom had got over Tamar's rape as easily as David himself seems to have done. In any case, David gave his blessing to Absalom's party and indeed explicitly allowed Amnon to go, while staying out of the way himself. David was devastated when he thought Absalom had killed all his half-brothers but Amnon's unpleasant co-conspirator Jonadab, presumably present at the feast, now sought to ingratiate himself with David by bringing reassurance. It was only Amnon that had been killed; and the implication of his comment about the rape is that Amnon deserved to die. Absalom avoided possible repercussions by fleeing to the protection of his (and Tamar's) grandfather in nearby Geshur – apparently then an independent province in the Golan Heights.

There are a lot of unanswered questions here. Was David expecting Absalom's action? Was his mourning (v 37) for Amnon or for Absalom? What did Tamar think of all this? What does seem clear is that the writer wants to raise questions in his readers' minds about David's failures in parenting and to make it plain that this was a dysfunctional family. Absalom's action is understandable, but whether it was right or wrong is left for readers to decide.

What do you think Absalom should have done in this situation? What advice would you have given? How significant do you think it is that God is not mentioned in this chapter?

---

[1] John 14:27

BIBLE IN A YEAR: Isaiah 37,38; Hebrews 4

2 Samuel 14

Deceit: Right or Wrong?

'...speaking the truth in love, we will in all things grow up into him who is the head, that is, Christ.'[1]

It is notable how often the same interests and concerns arise within the incidents recorded in these chapters. One can't help thinking that this is deliberate and that readers are being encouraged to ponder on these things. One theme is the repeated descriptions of manipulation and deceit, something with which we are only too familiar in these days of constant scams! David and Joab manipulate Uriah, causing his death. Nathan manipulates David to condemn himself through a story. Amnon deceives David and Tamar, causing her desolation. Absalom deceives David and Amnon, causing the latter's death and, here, Joab manipulates David, also using a story, causing Absalom's recall from Geshur. It is clear that deceit and manipulation from negative motives is not acceptable, but the question arises as to whether manipulation is OK when the motive is apparently good. There is no hint of any reservations about Nathan's methods, but this chapter is more ambiguous and the phrase 'life is complicated' comes to mind!

David gives in to Joab and sends for Absalom, but then refuses to see him for another two years. It is hard to see why David agrees to Absalom's return and then refuses to see him. When we read on and see the ongoing encounters between Joab and David, where Joab could be seen as exercising undue influence, it might be thought that David here is trying to prove that he is not totally under Joab's control, but this action gives time for Absalom both to develop further resentment of David and to increase his own popularity within the country. One can't help noticing both that Absalom uses strong manipulation to force Joab to influence David again and that Joab is able to do that, apparently fairly easily.

Should deceit or manipulation ever be used to bring about what we decide is right? If so, when? How likely are we to be manipulated, by friend or foe?

---

[1] Eph 4:15, TNIV

BIBLE IN A YEAR: **Isaiah 39,40; Psalm 106**

Divided Loyalties

'Bind us together Lord, / bind us together, / with cords that cannot be broken. / Bind us together Lord, / bind us together, / O bind us together in love.'[1]

The story in this chapter is skilfully told, packed full of ambiguities and questions. Should we start with the assumption that Absalom was a wicked usurper who deserved everything he got? There is no doubt that Absalom was conspiring – deceit and manipulation again in evidence – not just to succeed David, but to replace him. He was clearly attractive and gifted. He used his charms, first to demonstrate his royal credentials and then to show how he identified with, and cared about, the people: no wonder he won over their hearts. Perhaps we are being warned here about the danger of following celebrity leaders because they look good and flatter our egos. However, we know that the writer has also been identifying David's weaknesses. Perhaps Absalom saw himself as removing a king who had lost all credibility in failing to bring justice. Absalom's claim about his own policies does indicate a deficiency on David's part. He had clearly become bored with his military responsibilities; had he also become bored with pronouncing on legal cases? Perhaps we are being warned against resting on laurels and forgetting why the laurels were originally won. Blame is not always in one place!

David fled the city, temporarily removed from power, but still with many loyal supporters. His trust in God is once more demonstrated. He refused to allow the Ark of God to accompany him. If God wanted him to be deposed, fine; if not, the Ark would still be there when he came back to the city. It is worthwhile looking at the whole story of David and noticing how many of the positive things we remember about him, like this one, happened when he was removed from power and how few when he was in power.

Lord, we don't want leaders appointed for their celebrity or flattery, but nor do we want leaders who have forgotten their responsibilities. Help us to lead, and be led, well.

[1] B Gilman, 1974

BIBLE IN A YEAR: Isaiah 41,42; Hebrews 5

2 Samuel 16

Searching for Truth?

Thomas asked, 'How can we know the way?' Jesus answered, 'I am the way and the truth and the life. No one comes to the Father except through me.'[1]

All of us can identify with the saying 'nobody is perfect' – and most of us also with Paul's confession that even when he wants to do good he can end up doing bad things![2] The writer of 2 Samuel again wants us to recognise both sides of David's character. In 2 Samuel 9 we learned that David suddenly remembered the promise he had made, when the (now adult) Mephibosheth had been a small child, to look after Jonathan's family. This is usually told as a story of David's kindness but there seems little doubt that the writer has chosen to emphasise the length of time he took to think about his promise. Ziba and his family had been caring for the estate for all those years, but suddenly it was removed from them and given back to Mephibosheth, with apparently no compensation. Ziba now (vs 1–4) seeks recompense. He brings a large gift to David, professing full loyalty, and then (v 3) drops in an accusation, later

proved to be false,[3] that Mephibosheth had betrayed David. With no further investigation, David immediately believes him and hands all Saul's estate back to Ziba. Absalom's accusations about David's lack of concern for justice do seem to have some merit!

Verses 5–14, in contrast, show us a much more positive side of David's character. He is confronted by Shimei, a disturbed Saul supporter, who continually rants at and curses David. His own supporters want Shimei to be summarily executed but David refuses. He knows that curses are only meaningful if they are backed by God. He trusts God to work out his purposes and won't even presume that the ranting Shimei was not being used by God. David's knowledge of God always seems stronger than his knowledge of what God required from him as king!

'...Although I want to do good, evil is right there with me ... Who will rescue me ... Thanks be to God, who delivers me through Jesus Christ our Lord!'[4]

---

[1] John 14:5,6 [2] Rom 7:19 [3] 2 Sam 19:24–30 [4] Rom 7:21–25

BIBLE IN A YEAR: **Isaiah 43,44; Hebrews 6**

Advice Given and Rejected

'When Apollos wanted to go to Achaia, the believers encouraged him ... When he arrived, he was a great help to those who by grace had believed.'[1]

I expect that you, like me, know people who constantly ask for advice and listen to everyone but only stop asking when advice given corresponds to what they wanted to do anyway! We all need advice, but choosing good advisors, willing both to affirm and challenge us, is vital. Ahithophel and Hushai, two close advisors of David,[2] both came to advise Absalom. Hushai was there as a spy, but why Ahithophel deserted David is not as clear. It is possible he was Bathsheba's grandfather (both his son and Bathsheba's father were called Eliam,[3] a name not occurring elsewhere). If so, perhaps he had always felt resentful – another instance of David's earlier conduct having lasting consequences. Absalom had already taken Ahithophel's advice to assert dominance over David by sleeping with his concubines – Absalom's concern for his sister Tamar is not matched by any concern for these poor women. Neither Absalom nor David come out well in their use of women as power trophies, but that is not the writer's main concern here.

Ahithophel's good advice to catch David while on the run and unprepared was rejected in favour of Hushai's counsel to wait and prepare well. Knowing that this would lead to Absalom's defeat and the likelihood that he would be executed, we have the sad addendum that Ahithophel, being a responsible man, sorted out all his affairs and hanged himself. The campaign ended just as he predicted. The inclusion of Hushai's ambiguous comment that he will remain with 'the one chosen by the LORD'[4] perhaps indicates the writer's conviction that despite Absalom's gifts and David's deficiencies, it was David, not Absalom who was God's chosen leader. David's prayer that Ahithophel's advice be spurned[5] was answered by God (v 14). Absalom had apparently not thought that consulting God was necessary!

Think about whom you ask for advice, why you trust them and whether, or how, consulting God comes into the picture.

[1] Acts 18:27, TNIV [2] 1 Chr 27:33 [3] 2 Sam 11:3; 23:34 [4] 2 Sam 16:18 [5] 2 Sam 15:31

BIBLE IN A YEAR: **Isaiah 45,46; Psalm 107**

2 Samuel 18

Mixed Feelings

'But as for me, afflicted and in pain – may your salvation, God, protect me. I will praise God's name in song and glorify him with thanksgiving.'[1]

There are some football teams that always seem to perform better when they are facing the strongest opposition. David seems to follow a similar pattern! Relative military strength is yet to be tested, but Absalom had certainly been winning in the popularity stakes. Maybe that was what caused David to regain his enthusiasm, eager to retake control of his army. This time, however, the army was fighting not against an external enemy but in an internal leadership battle. If either Absalom or David died, the fight was immediately over. David's troops know that, this time, he will be more useful supporting from the rear – remembering that supporting from behind is very different from staying at home lounging around. It is always a challenge for leaders to make the right decision as to when to lead from the front and when from the rear. The battle happened; Absalom's plentiful but untrained irregulars were routed by David's well-trained standing army. Many thousands of the people David was supposed to have been leading were killed; as also, although this was against David's explicit command, was Absalom.

Questions are left in the air. Would that have happened if David had been fulfilling his responsibilities as well as he should? Would it have been possible for him to negotiate with Absalom before the fighting happened? Absalom's death would today be seen as a war crime: defenceless opponents should be captured but not murdered. Was Joab right or wrong to have had him killed? When we are told that everyone heard David's command (v 5), is this raising further issues of a power struggle between David and Joab? David was devastated. The news of victory was nothing beside the grief at the loss of his son.

Sometimes personal grief makes ministry responsibilities very difficult. Think about or discuss how you would help someone facing that kind of conflict of interest.

---

[1] Ps 69:29,30

BIBLE IN A YEAR: **Isaiah 47,48; Hebrews 7**

God: For or Against us?

'O make me understand it, / help me to take it in; / what it meant to thee, the Holy One, / to bear away my sin.'[1]

Here we have another 'lament psalm' that very definitely begins with a 'complaint' (v 1). This complaint is repeated many times in Scripture, not least in Jeremiah 12:1 'You are always righteous, LORD ... Yet I would speak with you about your justice: why does the way of the wicked prosper? Why do all the faithless live at ease?' Throughout the ages, believers and would-be believers have struggled with the question as to how a good and all-powerful God can let such terrible things happen. There are many answers that can be given, but few of them seem to convince one who has not yet personally encountered the living God. In this instance the psalmist wrestles not with a question from outside but with his own incomprehension and upset. It is good to know that this kind of questioning is affirmed rather than criticised!

The writer reflects on the fact that eventually these perverters of justice will be given their comeuppance by our just God: the 'when?' is left unanswered. 'All people' (v 9), both the boasting unjust and the questioning psalmist, will see this happening. The implication here is that it won't be in the way that either party really expected! 'All people will fear', but only the righteous 'will rejoice' (v 10)! We are often overwhelmed by particular circumstances, but once our focus moves away from what is happening to God himself, then our perspective changes. Whether or not the situation has changed, and there is no promise here or elsewhere that the timing of God's arrow against injustice will be soon, God is still there as our refuge. We can't rejoice in our circumstances, but we can 'rejoice in the LORD' (v 10). When the answer is eventually revealed, we will be able to 'glory in him'.

Give voice to any 'complaint' against God that you, or others, now have. Reflect on what you know of God and how you might 'take refuge in him' (v 10).

[1] KAM Kelly, 'Give Me a Sght, O Saviour', 1944

BIBLE IN A YEAR: Isaiah 49,50; Hebrews 8

2 Samuel 19:1–23

Starting Again?

'And this is his command: to believe in the name of his Son, Jesus Christ, and to love one another as he commanded us.'[1]

Some wars end with a negotiated peace settlement and some, as here, with victory and defeat. Both situations need careful handling on all sides. Particularly in a civil war, where both sides must continue to live together, minimising post-war effects on losers as well as winners is essential. We can all think of situations where disputes from centuries ago have an ongoing powerful influence on the attitudes of those left behind, who still see themselves on different sides. For us, with the privilege of hindsight, this chapter is as much a cautionary tale as an example. It raises questions for us to consider if ever faced by such circumstances. Perhaps that applies not just in the aftermath of war, but also after family or church disputes.

First (vs 1–8), we are presented with the issue of whether, how and when personal grief, which is obviously significant, should take precedence over leadership responsibilities. At first glance, the story seems to affirm Joab's conclusion that David had to concentrate on his own supporters. It is possible that we are being asked to consider whether David's grief for 'the opposition' could also have been harnessed in the reunification of the nation. Second, verses 9–23 deal with issues relating to defeated opponents. Here David shines. A significant part of Absalom's support came from Judah, David's own tribe. Winning them back was crucial. Appointing Amasa to lead David's own army was a brilliant strategy. Showing mercy to Shimei provided an encouragement to other previously vociferous opponents. Both stories involve Joab, now deposed by Amasa, whose brother, Abishai, has his advice rejected.

Lord, finding a way forward after serious and especially violent disagreements is so difficult. Please help us to search for solutions which can bring blessing to all sides.

---

[1] 1 John 3:23

BIBLE IN A YEAR: **Isaiah 51,52; Hebrews 9**

2 Samuel 19:24-43

The Rivals

Peter, seeing John, 'asked, "Lord, what about him?" Jesus answered, "If I want him to remain alive until I return, what is that to you? You must follow me."'[1]

I remember a TV advert picturing a well-dressed businessman walking quietly along a road and suddenly being assaulted by a youth in a hoodie. The camera then pulled back and revealed that the young man, seeing danger, had knocked the man out of the way of a falling pile of bricks, saving his life. The point was that only when seeing the bigger picture can you draw correct conclusions.

In chapter 16, David had heard Ziba's claim and immediately assumed that Mephibosheth was a traitor, but here we have Mephibosheth's side of the story with clear evidence that Ziba had been wrong, which means that David's original judgement had also been wrong. The text leaves the reader to decide whether David's current conclusion that Saul's estate should be shared between the two was an attempt to hide that wrong judgement or a realisation that both his decisions, first to give everything to Mephibosheth and secondly to take everything away from him, had been unjust. One hopes that it was the latter.

The next section of the chapter speaks of Barzillai, another person (like Jonathan) to whom David was indebted. The king was able to repay the debt by looking after a younger relative. The juxtaposition of these two stories is probably deliberate and again intended to raise questions in readers' minds! Lastly, we have more rivalry between David's tribe of Judah and the other northern tribes. The final sentence of the chapter shows that decisions were made not by working out the justice of the claims but by who made claims 'even more harshly'. The writer really does want his readers to assess what he is recording!

Have you ever made false judgements because of poor information? Has personal or tribal rivalry been your motivation? Pray for help to see the bigger picture, always seeking God's perspective.

[1] John 21:21,22

BIBLE IN A YEAR: **Isaiah 53,54; Psalms 108,109**

2 Samuel 20

Joab: Anti-Rebel or Rebel?

'Finally, brothers and sisters, rejoice! Strive for full restoration, encourage one another, be of one mind, live in peace. And the God of love and peace will be with you.'[1]

In recent years, governments have been faced with various crises with difficult decisions to be made. When should they wait and when should they act? Who should be cared for first? When should blame be placed or responsibility for wrong decisions accepted? This chapter is full of these kinds of questions, both for characters in the events recorded and for readers of the account. We are faced with the challenge of reading narratives, not just to note what happened but also to ask questions about the implications.

The background is another rebellion against David, led by Sheba the Benjaminite, which was overcome. The writer concentrates, however, on other matters. First, the plight of the 'ten concubines' (v 3): is this incidental or is the writer raising issues about the treatment of women? Is he emphasising David's unacceptable behaviour (clearly not in keeping with the law), or is he pointing out David's kindness? Then the interaction between the cousins: Amasa, Abishai and Joab were all sons of David's sisters. Was Amasa at fault or was David's timescale too short? Was David right to replace him so soon? He did, after all, reach the meeting point as soon as Joab! David, having deposed Joab, appointed Abishai instead, perhaps to avoid losing face, but the writer's comment 'Joab's men … went out under the command of Abishai' (v 7) is pointed. Joab would not tolerate being replaced by either Amasa or Abishai. His deceit and murder of Amasa was clearly wrong, but the omission of any further action by David is again notable. Finally, we have another story of a 'wise woman' (v 16) taking a leadership role in her town!

Do questions raised by this passage help us reassess the behaviour of our own leaders? Think about how this writer might describe actions and decisions you have taken recently!

---

[1] 2 Cor 13:11

BIBLE IN A YEAR: **Isaiah 55,56; Hebrews 10**

2 Samuel 21:1–14

Dealing with the Past

'Eternal Ruler of ... circling planets ... guide of the nations ... rule in our hearts, that we may ever be / guided and strengthened and upheld by thee.'[1]

It is fascinating to see how issues recur throughout history! Here we have an account of how David handled a situation where a historical injustice to a disadvantaged population was identified. There has been much discussion in recent years about whether and what kind of reparation should be made to those who have clearly been mistreated by previous regimes, often through colonialist activity, slave trading or different forms of racism. In this instance God makes it clear that current Israel is suffering because of a promise made in the distant past[2] and broken in the nearer past (v 2). It seems that God does see current regimes as responsible for keeping promises made by their predecessors and for making reparation to those mistreated by previous regimes. Apparently, responsibility cannot be avoided just because the current population was not directly involved in the actions.

However, God left David to decide what the recompense should be and again the writer appears to be pointing out difficulties with the actions he took. First, the Law gave various instructions about compensation, but allowing victims to choose the punishment, as David did, is not part of this. Their choice was to kill seven of Saul's descendants, which may have been convenient for David but went against the law that children should not be punished for their parents' sin.[3] Second, David himself had promised Saul that his descendants would not be killed.[4] It is ironic that his method of absolving the nation from the guilt of breaking a promise was to break another promise! The story of Rizpah's desperate grief at the death of her children seems to have been included to suggest that another solution should and could have been found.

Can you think of another way Gibeon could have been compensated? What might this story teach us about dealing with historical injustice or abuse?

[1] JW Chadwick, 'Eternal Ruler of the Ceaseless Round', 1864 [2] Josh 9 [3] Deut 24:16; cf Ezek 18
[4] 1 Sam 24:21,22

BIBLE IN A YEAR: Isaiah 57,58; Hebrews 11

2 Samuel 22:1–16

The God who Hears

'This is the confidence we have in approaching God: that if we ask anything according to his will, he hears us.'[1]

In recent chapters the writer has been raising many hard questions about David and the way he exercised his kingship. Perhaps the inclusion of this wonderful psalm, also found as Psalm 18, is to remind readers that David was a man of many parts. He may have had faults, but there is no doubt he was a godly poet who had, and was able to present, a powerful understanding of who God is and where David and his readers stand in relation to their great God. It is worth noting that this psalm was written right at the beginning of David's reign,[2] well before any of the events that we have been looking at recently. It is important for us to be realistic about our leaders, but here is a reminder to look beyond those leaders to God – and maybe to the good things that they have taught us about him.

Take time to read the whole psalm aloud and reflect on each phrase and the ways in which that might be, or might have been, a reality in your life. David knew God as strong and as safe, as one who protects (vs 2,3). He knew God as one who was always there, always ready, always listening and responding when David was experiencing circumstances which seem totally overwhelming and impossible to cope with (vs 4–7). He knew that God was not to be put in a box, not controlled by outside influences, but was himself controlling the universe (vs 8–16). David would have understood completely what CS Lewis meant in describing Aslan as 'not a tame lion'.[2] He knew that God heard him, but that any action taken would be entirely up to God and might not fit into his own presuppositions as to what God ought to be doing!

Lord, thank you so much for being my 'rock, in whom I take refuge' (v 3); for hearing my voice and listening to my cry; and for being you!

---

[1] 1 John 5:14 [2] See the heading to Ps 18 [3] CS Lewis, *The Lion, the Witch and the Wardrobe*

BIBLE IN A YEAR: **Isaiah 59,60; Psalms 110,111**

Subscribe to *Encounter with God* for just £16* annually

Take out or renew your subscription in three easy ways:

Online: su.org.uk/bible-guides **By phone:** 01908 856 000 **By post:** Complete this form and send it to **Freepost SU MAIL ORDER**

* Reduced cost for payments made by Direct Debit – saving you both time and money

Subscribe by post (please complete both sides of this form)

I want to take out an annual subscription to *Encounter with God* ☑

You will receive the next quarter's guide (October–December 2022 edition), and your annual subscription will renew on the date of first subscription. You can cancel at any time.

Title: _____   Full name: _____

Full address: _____

Postcode: _____

Tell us if you don't wish to receive postal updates:

We will send you updates about the difference you are making to children and young people's lives through your giving, and offer you further opportunities to ensure the good news is shared. However, if you would rather not receive such information, please tick here ☐

Tel. No. (Home): _____   Mobile No. _____

Email address: _____

Email contact: Please keep me updated on the latest resources from Scripture Union, please tick here ☐

Scripture Union will never sell your data or share it with another company or charity for marketing purposes. You can change the way we contact you at any time by contacting Scripture Union: 01908 856000, via our website or emailing hello@scriptureunion.org.uk. You can read our full privacy policy at: www.su.org.uk/privacy

Could you top up your subscription with a donation?

At Scripture Union, as well as producing Bible reading guides, we create opportunities for children and young people to explore the Bible and respond to Jesus. Your subscription is already helping to fund this vital work but through a top-up donation, you could help make even more impact. It's estimated that 95% of all under 18s in England and Wales don't go to church. Your gift could help us take the good news to even more of them!

A top-up gift of £4 could subsidise a child or young person's place at an SU camp
A top-up gift of £9 could gift children in a primary school class a children's Bible
A top-up gift of £20 could help an SU worker set up a new youth club in a deprived area

Add £4 ☐   Add £9 ☐   Add £15 ☐   Add £20 ☐   Add £ _____

Payment

If you choose to pay by Direct Debit, your subscription will cost just **£16**. If you prefer to pay by cheque or card, the cost for the year is **£19**. If you are able to top up your subscription with a donation, your gift will reoccur annually along with your subscription (unless you let us know otherwise). Thank you.

Note: *This form is for UK subscriptions only. For overseas subscriptions, see su.org.uk/bible-guides*

Please fill in the relevant section below based on your preferred method of payment:

Bank details

Instruction to your Bank or Building Society to pay by Direct Debit.

DIRECT Debit

NAME & FULL POSTAL ADDRESS OF YOUR BANK OR BUILDING SOCIETY

To: The Manager Bank / Building Society Name:

Full address:

Postcode:

Name(s) of Account Holder(s):

Bank or Building Society Account Number:

Bank Sort Code:

Service User Number (SUN): 8 4 0 6 5 1

Reference number: (for office use)

Instruction to Your Bank or Building Society

Please pay Scripture Union Direct Debits from the account detailed in this instruction subject to the safeguards assured by the Direct Debit Guarantee. I understand that this Instruction may remain with Scripture Union and, if so, details will be passed electronically to my Bank or Building Society.

Signature(s):

Date: D D M M Y Y

Note: Banks and Building Societies may not accept Direct Debits instructions for some types of accounts.

Pay for your subscription by cheque or card payment

Subscription cost **£19**   Optional top up donation £   Total cost £

Cheque payable to Scripture Union ☐   WRITE YOUR CHEQUE NUMBER HERE   Postal order ☐

Please debit my credit/debit card ☐

Card no:

Issue no/valid from: /   Expiry date: /   Security no:

Card holder's Signature:

Date: D D M M Y Y

REVEALING JESUS

Revealing Jesus is a new mission framework from Scripture Union, designed to help you journey into faith with the **95%** of children and young people not in church.

FIND OUT MORE: SU.ORG.UK/REVEALINGJESUS

ENCOUNTER
WITH GOD

Bible readings for July–September 2022

2 Samuel 3-9
Andy Robinson

Luke 3-9
Daniel McGinnis

Numbers 20-36
Tanya Ferdinandusz

1 Timothy
Jonny Libby

2 Samuel 10-24
Mary Evans

SUPPORTING SU's MISSION

TO SHARE
THE GOOD
NEWS WITH
THE NEXT
GENERATION

SUPPORTING SU's MISSION

www.scriptureunion.org.uk

ISBN 978 1 78506 855 3

9 781785 068553

**Scripture
Union**

www.scriptureunion.org.uk
Encounter with God Jul–Sept 2022